HEINEMANN HISTORY

EDUCATION SINCE 1700

ROBERT HUME

Head of History, Clarendon House School, Ramsgate

HEINEMANN
EDUCATIONAL

Heinemann Educational,
a division of Heinemann Educational Books Ltd,
Halley Court, Jordan Hill, Oxford OX2 8EJ

OXFORD   LONDON   EDINBURGH
MELBOURNE   SYDNEY   AUCKLAND
IBADAN   NAIROBI   GABORONE   HARARE
KINGSTON   PORTSMOUTH NH (USA)
SINGAPORE   MADRID

First published 1989

British Library Cataloguing in Publication Data

Hume, Robert
  Education since 1700.
  1. Great Britain. Education 1700–1985. For
  schools.
  I. Title
  370'.941

ISBN 0-435-31040-2

Designed and produced by
The Pen & Ink Book Company Ltd, Huntingdon

Printed in Great Britain by Scotprint, Edinburgh

To my students – past, present and future

Acknowledgements

The author and publisher would like to thank the following for
permission to reproduce photographs on the pages indicated:

Barnaby's Picture Library: p. 38; BBC Enterprises Ltd for the
cartoon taken from *Measurement in Education* (1974) by Douglas
Pidgeon and David Allen: p. 56. The British Library: pp.6 (left), 20
and 21; The Dean and Chapter of Canterbury: p. 4; Rev. Charles P.
Gordon Clark for the photograph taken from *The Story of the Church
of King Charles the Martyr, Royal Tunbridge Wells* p. 6 (middle);
Format: p. 61; Greater London Record Office (Maps and Prints):
pp. 18 and 19; Guildhall Library, City of London: p. 23; The Hulton
Picture Company: pp. 26, 27 (lower), 40 (top) and 52; The
Illustrated London News Picture Library: pp. 41 and 50 (lower);
Margaret Lawrence: p. 46; Leicester University Press for the
photograph taken from *School Architecture* by E.R. Robson: p. 40
(lower); Lewisham Local History Centre: p. 14; Manchester Local
History Library: p.32; The Master of Eastbridge Hospital, Kent: p. 7
(left); National Monuments Record: p. 24 (lower); National
Museum of Wales (Welsh Folk Museum): p. 6 (top); Punch
Publications: pp. 37, 39 and 42; Royal Commission of the Historical
Monuments of England: p.24 (lower); The Royal Museum and Art
Gallery: p. 24 (middle); The late David Scurrell: p. 30; Shropshire
Libraries Local Studies Department: p. 27 (top); Society of
Antiquaries of London: p. 15; SPCK: p. 12; St. Leonard's Archives:
p. 17; The *Times Educational Supplement*: p. 56 (lower); University of
Exeter: p. 6 (right); University of Keele: p. 58 (top).

The author and publisher would like to thank Malcolm Seaborne
for permission to reproduce a photograph from his book *The
English School: its Architecture and Organisation 1370–1870*: p.5.

We have been unable to contact the copyright holder of the
photograph which appears on page 50 (top) and would be grateful
for any information which would enable us to do so.

Details of Written Sources

In some sources the wording or sentence structure has been
simplified to make sure that the source is accessible.

J. Bentham, *Principles of Penal Law*, 1802: 3.2F
C. Bingham, *A Picture of Life, 1872–1940*, John Murray 1941: 3.6E
Canterbury Cathedral Library Churchwarden's Presentments 1716:
2.4F
W. Cobbett, The *Political Register*, 21 September 1833: 3.2G
S. J. Curtis and M. E. A. Boultwood, *An Introductory History of
English Education Since 1800*, University Tutorial Press 1970: 3.2A–E
Gloucester Journal, 3 November 1783: 2.5C
Thomas Hughes, *Tom Brown's Schooldays*, Puffin 1971: 2.10C
Eric James, *Education and Leadership*, Harrap 1951: 4.2G
K. Harry Ree, *The Essential Grammar School*, Harrap 1956: 4.2I
SPCK Archives: 2.4E
D. Salmon (ed.), *The Practical Parts of Lancaster's Improvements and
Bell's Experiments*, Cambridge University Press 1932: 2.6B
Shropshire Record Office: 2.5A, 2.5D, 2.5F
J. Simon 'Was There a Charity School Movement?' The
Leicestershire Evidence, in B. Simon (ed.), *Education in
Leicestershire, 1540–1940*, Leicester University Press 1968: 2.4B
W. E. Tate, 'SPCK Archives', *Archives III*, 1957: 2.4A

The author and publisher would like to thank Times Newspapers
Ltd for permission to reproduce extracts from the following articles
which appear on p. 63:

'First Rebuffs for Advocates of Opting Out' and 'Parent Power
Comes Under State Control' which originally appeared in *The
Times Educational Supplement* on 6/1/89 and 11/9/87.

CONTENTS

1.1 THE NATIONAL PICTURE

The quality of education provided in British schools is today an important political issue, but it has not always been so. People in the past were often completely uninterested in it. In a mainly agricultural society, a farm labourer or a domestic servant had to pick up only the specific skills needed for the job, and would have found learning to read and write rather unnecessary. Schooling was often just fitted in between bouts of more serious work, and only a minority of the population had much education.

The traditional picture of education before 1700 has been a depressing one of, apparently, only a very small number of schools. Historians have usually drawn attention to **public schools** and prominent **grammar schools** (often established during the reigns of Edward VI and Elizabeth I) but to little else. This is because, in trying to estimate the number of schools in existence, historians have tended to rely solely on one book (Christopher Wase's *Survey of the Free Grammar Schools*, 1678) and, more often still, on the Church of England's subscription books and licences, as in Source A.

At the Restoration of the monarchy in 1660, the Church of England had started to sell compulsory licences to schoolteachers.

SOURCE **A**

The master of the Queen's School (now known as the King's School) Canterbury, swears to the oaths and signs his name, 31 July 1714. ▼

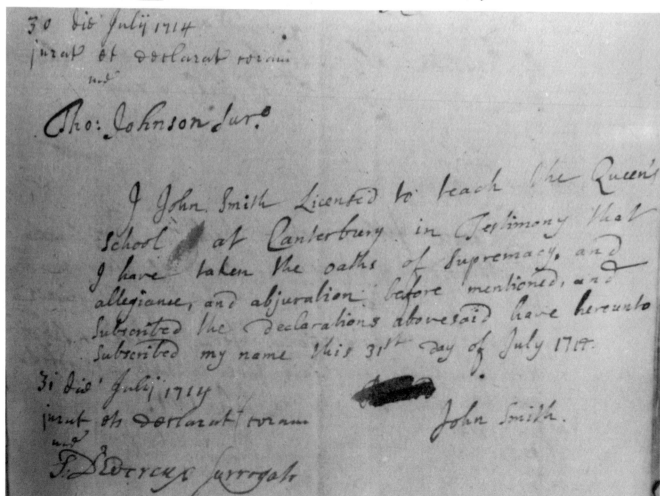

SOURCE **B**

Archbishop James Margetson, founder of Drighlington School, Yorkshire, 1671.

The church was worried that **Nonconformists** (those who did not conform to the teachings of the Church of England) might be appointed. Until 1702, every schoolteacher, in no matter how small a school, was meant to swear an oath of loyalty to the church and the king. In the records where these teachers signed their names, their schools are called either 'free schools', or 'grammar schools', or 'English writing schools', or 'public schools'.

Grammar schools taught classical subjects, like Latin and Greek, to children – often free of charge. This was possible because many of these schools had been left a sum of money in a rich person's will. This money was controlled by a group of trustees who were sometimes members of a London company, such as the Haberdashers or Skinners.

Public schools also taught classics, but were much more exclusive places which had full control over their own affairs. Due to the considerable fees charged, only the sons of the very rich could be educated at these schools.

The long-standing schools reported in these records tend to be found in two different kinds of community. First, they were present in places where a large number of people lived (such as market and county towns). Here, prosperous tradespeople could be found who were able to leave money in their wills to set up schools, or at least pay a small subscription during their lifetime. There were also newly rich merchant families who saw schooling as a way of improving themselves socially, to the point where they were on a level with the traditional ruling classes.

Schools were also listed in parishes which had the good fortune of receiving help from donors. Such donors had either provided a school in their will, or already set the school on some firm footing during their lifetime.

Permanent schools were rarer in the countryside, where the main activity was working on the land. However, certain church records, such as bishops' court documents, show that little schools in quite small villages were forever being set up, only to peter out again on the death of the benefactor, or on the teacher's own death. Many of these successfully managed to escape the eye of the church authorities when they were checking up on abuses.

In fact, recent local evidence suggests that before 1700 there were far more schools in existence than are normally reported in the standard histories of education. If we take the county of Shropshire, for example, even in the tiny parish of Ludford in the south there were a number of people 'teaching Children to read' in 1662; at Middleton Scriven 'there is a poore man . . . the which is olde & lame & one that canott doe any thinge else towards gettinge him a livelyhood by teachinge two ore three boys or childrin'; at Greet there was 'onely a poore woman that teaches to spell and read part of the yeare'; while at Burford there were 'one or two petty schools to teach Children to spell & read a little'. All these were schools which taught poor children, even though such schools are generally treated as virtually non-existent before the early eighteenth century.

1.2 THE EVIDENCE HISTORIANS USE

EVIDENCE

Have you ever tried to complete a jigsaw puzzle when several of the pieces are missing? It can be a disappointment not to be able to see the entire picture.

Now imagine the greater disappointment when, after hours of work on a jigsaw, you find towards the end that not just a few but a very considerable number of pieces, which would have given detail and meaning to the picture, are in fact missing. This is the kind of problem which historians face as they collect and sift through their evidence to try and build up a picture of education before 1700.

A shortage of evidence

Why is there such a shortage of evidence? First, apart from the public schools and the well-established grammar schools, the majority of schools at this time were not permanent and did not have special buildings. Instead, they were informal relationships between about a dozen children (usually boys) and teachers. These came into existence when a teacher arrived in a village, and vanished when the teacher left or died, or when the children were needed at home. Classes were usually held either in a distant part of the church, such as the vestry room or a chapel, or in the teacher's own home.

Secondly, not only have these schools left no buildings behind for historians to examine, but they have left very few, if any, written records of their own to show us what their day-to-day running was like. Headteachers did not keep **log books** (regular records) until 1862. Only if a school had been left a large sum of money, or if it had a regular subscription to collect in and spend, were records of managers' meetings kept.

So how do historians find out about schools before 1700? All schoolmasters and schoolmistresses were supposed to buy a licence from their bishop before they began work. In theory, historians should be able to use their **subscriptions** (or

A horn book, from which pupils would learn the letters of the alphabet.

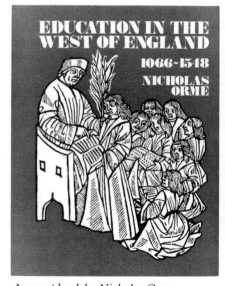

EDUCATION IN THE WEST OF ENGLAND
1066–1548
NICHOLAS ORME

A recent book by Nicholas Orme.

The School House, Milton, Gravesend, Kent, built in 1580.

The King Charles Chapel, Tunbridge Wells. A school was held in the gallery during the summer months until 1812.

Rules to be observed by the schoolmaster at the Eastbridge Hospital School, Canterbury, Kent, founded in 1584.

signatures) in the record books at the time the licence was granted to them, to get an idea of the number of schools in existence. In practice, we know that only those teaching at the more wealthy, older, grammar schools could afford, or took the trouble, to buy a licence. This is because we have hundreds of references to schoolteachers being taken before bishops' courts and fined for not having a licence. These 'citations' prove that there were a huge number of parishes with small schools at this early date.

Bishops also sent out questionnaires, known as '**inquiries**', to their clergy. One of the questions asked whether there was a school in the parish. The answers reveal many 'poor', 'lame' and blind men and women teaching in schools.

To obtain more evidence, historians have to hunt down every chance reference possible to schools. For the more wealthy teachers, their **wills** and **inventories** (lists) of goods, where they survive, are useful for telling us about their possessions and life-style. **Records** kept by the clergy – vestry minutes and churchwardens' accounts – sometimes mention repairs made to a school held in the church. **Diaries** and **autobiographies** contain references to small schools. **Memorial stones** can show **endowments** (sums of money) given to set up schools; and even **gravestones** (Source F) can contain useful information to help complete the picture.

EXERCISE

1 Group the six sources on these two pages into (a) primary sources and (b) secondary sources for studying education before 1700. Give reasons for your answers.

2 The following statement appeared in an unpublished essay on education: 'As you can see from Source B, by no means every school in these days had a special building.' Would you say that the writer had reached a reasonable conclusion?

3 a What subjects does the tombstone (Source F) suggest that John Cade taught at his school in Beckenham?

   b Is more, or less, variety offered to his pupils by the schoolmaster at Eastbridge Hospital (Source E)?

4 What, if anything, does Source E show us about how schoolmasters actually behaved?

5 'Because Source C is a primary source, it must be much more reliable than Source D, which is only a secondary source.' Do you agree? Explain your answer carefully.

SOURCE E

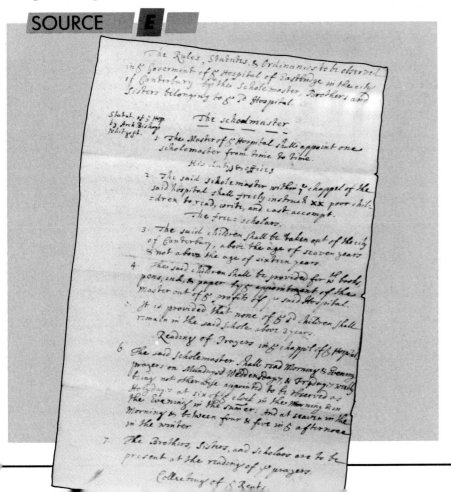

SOURCE F

Tombstone of Beckenham schoolmaster John Cade.

2.1 FROM PATERNALISM TO LAISSEZ-FAIRE

EMPATHY

In 1640 Parliament launched an inquiry into the advantages of the government organizing a system of education in England. Some people were in favour of the government providing schools for the poor. One speaker demanded financial assistance for poor children of school age. Another claimed that the state should charge a rate for education services. At the same time, it was suggested that new universities could supplement Oxford and Cambridge. These proposals show a concern for education which had existed throughout the reigns of Elizabeth I and James I. This caring attitude is often described as **paternalism** because it is rather like the caring relationship between a father and child.

During Cromwell's Protectorate further grants of money for education were made. But government support for education came to a halt at the Restoration in 1660. During this time the grammar schools were seen as places where Puritan and anti-royalist ideas could be spread. No more money was given for instruction in basic skills such as reading, writing and simple arithmetic. The result of this change in attitude was that during the eighteenth and nineteenth centuries responsibility for education was left to the church or to the patronage of wealthy individuals.

The leading economist of the eighteenth century, **Adam Smith**, unconsciously encouraged the government in its 'hands-off', approach to education. In his book, *An Inquiry into the Nature and Causes of the Wealth of Nations* (1776), Smith made a strong attack on all types of government regulation. He was not alone in thinking that the best kind of government is that which governs least. This idea came to be known as *laissez-faire* – leaving people alone to do what they think is best. Some of those who thought in a similar way claimed that it was against the will of God for governments to interfere with how God had originally made things. Others, who did not believe in *laissez-faire*, argued that while the fittest and richest could survive, the idea did nothing for the poor.

Smith's theories continued to gain popularity among those who believed that economic progress would best be achieved by non-interference. This meant no taxes or duties on goods, and less control over workers. In mainland Europe, meanwhile, government restrictions were strengthened, not reduced, during the eighteenth century.

According to Smith, the government's role should be restricted to defending the country in time of war and to providing for the public's welfare. Smith himself believed that education, public health and assistance for the needy should not be neglected. However, in the late eighteenth century the government preferred to take a more extreme *laissez-faire* line, and was unwilling to interfere in what it said were the private affairs of the individual. It tried instead to get people to stand on their own two feet.

The government's *laissez-faire* policy was not the only reason for England's late start in organizing a system of national education. There was also no special urgency to introduce a

SOURCE A

Adam Smith, 1723–90.

SOURCE B

'What are the duties of the Government? Generally speaking, to maintain the frame of society; to restrain violence and crime, to protect person and property, to enact and administer the laws needful for the maintenance of peace, order, and justice, to sanction public works as docks, harbours, canals, railways etc.

'It is not the duty of Government to feed the people, to clothe them, to build houses for them, to direct their industry or their commerce, to superintend their families, to cultivate their mind, to shape their opinions, or to supply them with religious teachers, physicians, schoolmasters, books and newspapers.

'These are things that the people can and ought to do for themselves.

Edward Baines, writing about state education in 1846.

EMPATHY

system in England at this time. France and Prussia, on the other hand, did develop early national education systems. In these countries, schools were considered important, first, for training soldiers for war and, secondly, for turning out respectful, obedient citizens.

A long series of English governments took no interest in the field of education during the whole of the eighteenth century and well into the nineteenth. Education was seen as an unnecessary luxury, the benefits of which took a long time to appear. The establishment of schools was left entirely in the hands of wealthy individuals, the church and enterprising men and women until 1833.

Laissez-faire.

EXERCISE

1 A successful school which takes pupils whose parents pay fees, as well as local children from poorer families who do not pay a fee, has been burnt down.
   a How do you think a paternalist government would react to an appeal from the school for money to rebuild?
   b How do you think a *laissez-faire* government would react to an appeal from the school for money to rebuild?

2 a What services does the government today provide for its citizens?
   b How would you expect a paternalist to react to this?
   c How would you expect a supporter of *laissez-faire* to react to this?

2.2 SCHOOLS FOR THE POOR

Education can have a number of different purposes: it can make people feel happier and more fulfilled; it can give training in a skill which will be useful for work as an adult; it can help develop civilized and social behaviour; and it can improve people's employment chances. During the eighteenth century, however, the usefulness of education for training people in skills was less valued than its use for disciplining the poor.

Many schools were set up in response to what was believed to be a **decline in morals** among the population. In particular, the poor were blamed for increasing idleness, crime and prostitution. Schooling was offered as a way to improve moral standards among the 'lower classes' by teaching better behaviour to their children.

Human society was very rigidly classified at this time. It was thought best by those with power in society that, while some people were born to rule, the majority were born only to work and obey. The poor were considered to be the lowest level of the social pyramid, and their lowly status could not be changed. 'God so orders it that we have always some Poor among us,' wrote one bishop in 1720.

Since the end of the seventeenth century, people of higher social rank believed that the poor were becoming restless and

The 'Great Chain of Being'. Everyone was said to be born into their place in the chain. ▼

SOURCE A

'The deficiency of education among the lower classes is greatly to be regretted, many being unable to read, and still more of course to write or keep accounts. This is productive of much inconvenience to the individuals, unfitting them for many situations, for which their natural abilities might otherwise qualify them, and leaving them an easy target to numerous temptations.'

H. E. Strickland writing in support of educating the lower classes, 1812.

SOURCE B

'It would teach them to despise their lot in life, instead of making them good servants in agriculture and other employment. It would enable them to read seditious pamphlets, vicious books and publications against Christianity; it would render them insolent to their superiors.'

Davies Giddy M.P. speaking in a debate in Parliament in 1807, against educating the lower classes.

less willing to accept their position in society. Parish priests reported a general deterioration in manners and morals. More and more offenders were brought before the bishops' courts accused of working on Sundays, lying, fighting in the churchyard, swearing, drunkenness and adultery.

A century before, the Elizabethans had made a distinction between two types of poor. First, there were the **impotent poor**, who were unfit to work and so poor through no fault of their own. Secondly, there were the **able-bodied poor**, who chose not to work through laziness. The impotent poor were thought to deserve help or relief. In helping them, the **poor rates** – the money collected from better-off people in the parish – had to keep in line with the price of bread. As the poor rates rose, some people returned to their old prejudices about the poor being poor simply because they were unwilling to work hard. The philosopher John Locke, for example, blamed a trebling of the poor rate in thirty years on the poor not receiving proper discipline or moral education.

The ruling classes came to believe more and more that poor children had to be better trained for their very basic role in society. At all costs, they must not become a burden on the rates. This was the thinking behind the **charity schools**, also known as **day schools**, that were founded at this time with money provided by wealthy people.

Training for life

As well as teaching 'acceptable' behaviour, the education provided in these schools was aimed to help children develop a skill. (See Source D, Unit 2.3.)

Far-sighted people saw schooling as an investment. It could provide both talent and labour to fight in the army and navy. These things would bring great benefit to the country. In the words of one writer about 1730, it was 'folly to imagine that Great and Wealthy Nations can subsist' without most of the poor being adequately trained and employed.

Care had to be taken not to give these charity children too big ideas about themselves, so as to over-qualify them for very humble employment. With this in mind, only a few would be taught writing and to do accounts. The majority were to be taught merely spelling and reading, Scripture and the Ten Commandments. On top of this, all were trained in a skill, such as gardening or making hop-sacks. Their time at school was not intended to help them to improve their social position. Rather, it was meant to get everyone working at their best under the existing system.

These charity schools existed side by side with private schools which taught accounts and book-keeping, qualifying middle-class boys for trade and business. Meanwhile, with the rich in mind, dancing and fencing lessons were offered to 'young gentlemen', and dancing, fine embroidery and deportment lessons were available for 'young ladies' seeking a 'fortunate' marriage.

2.3 REASONS FOR THE DAY SCHOOLS

CAUSATION

Day schools with free places for the poor could be found in England since Elizabethan times. Nevertheless, after 1660, and even more so in the early eighteenth century, many more such schools were founded than ever before. Why was this?

The eighteenth century is often called the 'age of benevolence', or the **'age of philanthropy'** (good works), and it is true that some men and women setting up schools had very honourable intentions (Sources A and B). Among their number must be included those few who gave money anonymously, with no thought of being remembered by future generations.

As the number of poor continued to rise, however, the government was forced to realize that a large and discontented population posed a possible threat to peace in the country. A few people still thought that educating the poor was dangerous because it would make them get ideas 'above themselves'. But the government and church came to believe that something had to be done to improve the morals of the poorer classes (Source C). The poor had to be educated to accept the drudgery of their day-to-day existence. So they had to be taught only what was required of them for a useful working life (Source D).

Those who gave money to set up the schools (the **donors**) sometimes did so because they felt they had a duty towards the poor on their estates or in their local village. That is why they made the condition that only local children should be allowed to attend their school (Sources A and B).

Some modern writers, however, believe that these wealthy landowners could have done much more for the poor. Compared to their huge incomes, they actually donated very little. Nor did trades-people and shopkeepers in the towns keep up their enthusiasm towards charity schools into the second quarter of the eighteenth century (Source E).

In fact, the motives of many of the early benefactors of these schools were full of self-interest. In some cases, people firmly laid down in their will that their name should be used in the title of the school (such as Lady Thornhill's School, Wye, Kent), or in the naming of the scholars (for example, the 'Langfordian boys' at Ludlow, Shropshire). Others asked that their name be inscribed on stone at the front of their building, or on a plaque in the parish church (Source G).

One prosperous Shrewsbury draper, James Millington, was more self-seeking still. In his will of 1734 he required that a portrait of himself be placed in the schoolroom. Like many other donors up and down the country, he directed also that a special sermon be preached on the anniversary of his death, so that his charitable gift would never be forgotten.

The benefactors of the charity day schools, then, contributed to schools for a tremendous variety of reasons. It would be quite wrong to label the donors collectively either as philanthropists or as selfish egotists.

SOURCE

'. . . to help the poor honest Industrious Inhabitants of Church Aston, who have more Children than they are able to provide for.'

Mrs Mary Broughton, explaining in her will why she was endowing a school in Church Aston, Shropshire, 1728.

SOURCE

'. . . to putt to schoole such poore Children inhabiting in the parish of Hartlip as rents shall be sufficient to maintaine at such schoole.'

Extract from the will of Mary Gibbon, of Hartlip, Kent, 1678.

SOURCE

A FORM of a Subscription for a CHARITY-SCHOOL.

Subscription form for donating to a charity school. (This was the standard form sent out by the Society for Promoting Christian Knowledge (SPCK) in the early eighteenth century.)

SOURCE

'. . . If due care be taken in the establishing Free Schools for Educating the Children of the poor . . . we may always be furnished with a Nursery of able seamen, pilots, Engineers & indeed of men of the greatest abilities in Every science.'

Letter to the Society for Promoting Christian Knowledge from a lawyer called Hook, c. 1700.

SOURCE E

'So selfish and unwilling to do good are those with us, that I fear we shall not be able long to support our charity school. Some time ago, we had 10 pounds subscribed, but some are already weary and withdraw, and indeed there is amongst us a strange want of religious zeal and publick spiritedness.'

A charity school running out of funds. Thomas Watts, the SPCK's agent in Orpington, writing to headquarters, 30 May 1718.

SOURCE

Estimates of population from the Compton Census (1676)			
a Fordwich	190	g Boughton Monchelsea	282
b Walmer	167	h Faversham	2,000
c Wye	333	i Loose	283
d Ashford	1,667	j Lewisham	983
e Cranbrook	2,167	k Yalding	1,163
f Hawkhurst	1,667	l Tonbridge	1,957

A map of Kent just before 1700. Those parishes which are shaded have schools. Population figures of some of these are shown in the table.

SOURCE G

DEO GLORIA
THIS SCHOOL WAS ERECTED
ANNO 1694 AT Yͤ SOLE CHARGE
OF EDWARD PHILLIPS
NATIUE OF THIS PARISH CITISEN
& MERCHANT TAYLER OF
LONDON FOR THE FREE
SCHOOLING OF 12 POOR PARISH
BOYS TO READ & WRITE WITH
A BIBLE & OTHER BOOKS TO BE
GIUEN TO EACH BOY BY THE
FOUNDER FOR EVER

SOURCE H

'. . . that the said poor children shall wear on their upper garment the crest of me, John Roan.'

Extract from John Roan's will, 1643. Roan founded the Grey Coat School, Greenwich, Kent.

◀ *Inscription to the memory of Edward Phillips at The Old School, St Martin's, Shropshire.*

EXERCISE

1 What common motive do you think Mary Broughton and Mary Gibbon (Sources A and B) had in providing schools?

2 Is there any connection between places with schools and the population figures in Source F?

3 'The rich felt sorry for poor people who could not afford to send their children to school.' Is this a sufficient reason to explain why men and women in the eighteenth century provided the poor with schools which they could go to virtually free of charge?

4 'Despite what they may have said, the real reason people provided schools was to make a name for themselves.' Do you agree?

5 Would it have made any difference if the rich had not volunteered money to set up schools for the poor? Explain your answer carefully.

2.4 THE CHARITY SCHOOLS DEBATE

EVIDENCE

Most school books about the history of education tell us that during the first quarter of the eighteenth century a new kind of school for the poor, called a **charity school**, came into being. They go on to say that these schools, which were set up all over England and Wales, were organized by the London-based **Society for Promoting Christian Knowledge**, the **SPCK**.

Schools sponsored by the SPCK were intended to give children a basic grounding in reading, writing and arithmetic, and to teach them the Christian catechism by heart. Nothing further was thought to be suitable, in case these children should become over-ambitious or rebellious. Unlike earlier schools, we are told, the charity schools were financed by small-scale subscriptions from tradespeople and shopkeepers, together with collections held at an annual charity sermon.

Although most writers agree that a few schools for poor children were already in existence, they view what happened during the first quarter of the eighteenth century as a new initiative, and speak of a **charity school movement**, co-ordinated by the SPCK.

New evidence

In the past twenty years, these views have been challenged. It is still believed that the SPCK was closely involved in the setting up of the London charity schools; but historians examining Leicestershire and Kent have discovered documentary and physical evidence proving that there were a large number of schools educating the poor long before the SPCK began in 1698.

Some of these schools (such as at Narborough in Leicestershire and at Tunbridge Wells in Kent) were kept going by small contributions made by local tradespeople. So this method of finance was not completely new. Also, most of the schools built in the early eighteenth century had no connection whatever with the SPCK, and the society could not have known of their existence. Not only did most schools never correspond with it, but there is no evidence that they used the SPCK's recommended books or taught the catechism in the recommended fashion. The schools often went outside the 7 to 11 age range of children which the SPCK advised. In many cases, too, the curriculum, instead of being restricted to reading, writing and arithmetic, included locally useful skills like navigation and hop-bagging.

Recent research findings also contradict the traditional view of what happened to children when they left charity schools. The widespread belief is that most boys would, on leaving, be apprenticed by the schools' trustees. As **apprentices**, they would live with a master, who would teach them a trade or craft. However, from local evidence it appears that only a few charity schools could afford to apprentice children, because of the growing expense of an apprenticeship which lasted seven years. Charity schools, in fact, could barely afford to pay a teacher's salary and the rent, furnishing and heating of the schoolroom. The truth is that many children had no choice but to return to their parents on leaving school.

SOURCE A

The Society for Promoting Christian Knowledge (SPCK) was 'the founder of the English system of national education. Nothing was too small for the society's attention, and no task was too great for it to undertake.'

W. E. Tate, in an article assessing the importance of the SPCK.

SOURCE B

'The SPCK was not well informed about what went on outside London'; in Leicestershire, the SPCK 'appears to have made only a slight and temporary impact'.

J. Simon, 'Was There a Charity School Movement?', 1968.

QUESTIONS

1 To what extent does the new evidence about charity schools disagree with the traditional view?

2 Is there enough new evidence to overturn the traditional view? What more — if anything — needs to be found out?

SOURCE C

The Dean Stanhope School, Deptford, 1871.

SOURCE D

An engraving showing boys and girls from London charity schools in the Strand, at their national thanksgiving for the Peace of Utrecht, 7 July 1713. About four thousand children lined the galleries.

SOURCE E

'I. That they constantly attend the School, from the hours of 7 to 11 in the Morning, and from 1 to 5 in the Evening, the Summer Half-Year; and from 8 to 11 in the Morning, and from 1 to 4 in the Evening, the Winter Half-Year.

'II. That they teach them the True Spelling of Words, make them Mind their stops, and bring them to read slowly and distinctly.

'III. That the Children be taught to Write a fair legible Hand, with the Grounds of Arithmetick; and that the Girls be taught to Knit their Stockings and Gloves, and to Mark, Sew, mend their Cloathes, Spin . . .

'IV. That they make it their chief Business to instruct the Children in the Principles of the Christian Religion, as professed in the Church of England, and laid down in the Church Catechism.'

'Orders to be Observed by the Masters and Mistresses', c.1700.

SOURCE F

'Our Schoolmaster John Hassell did not at all for several months last past bring his Children to Church, as he used, & ought to do . . . for being very negligent in his duty, & for absenting himself from his Scholars in school hours.'

The churchwardens of Cranbrook, Kent, draw the attention of the Archbishop of Canterbury to a negligent schoolmaster in their parish, June 1716. This school never appears in the SPCK's annual lists of schools.

EXERCISE

1   Are the following sources primary or secondary for studying charity schools? For each one, give a reason for your decision.

   a A textbook by M. G. Jones, *The Charity School Movement*, published in 1938.

   b A piece of plain knitting done by a girl at the Greenwich Blue Coat School.

   c A list of tradespeople subscribing to the Shrewsbury Public Subscription School, 1708.

   d A model of the St Andrew's charity school in London.

   e R. B. Jones's *Economic and Social History of England, 1770–1978*, published in 1979.

Could any of the sources which you have marked as secondary become a primary source for something quite different at some time in the future?

2   **a** Study Source F. 'Boys and girls attending charity schools in England in the eighteenth century would not have had a good education.' Do you agree? Explain.

   b Does Source E support the evidence in Source F?

3   Look at Source D. Do you think it is a reliable piece of evidence? Give your reasons.

4   A photograph of physical evidence, like Source C, cannot be biased. Will it be of more use to historians than other kinds of evidence?

5   **a** Does Source D support the traditional view of charity schools, or the new evidence?

   b Which view does Source F tie in with?

2.5 SUNDAY SCHOOLS

EMPATHY

Robert Raikes, a Gloucester newspaper owner, is still often given credit for pioneering Sunday schools in the 1780s. This is a mistaken view. There had been many attempts to set up schools earlier in the eighteenth century, particularly by the Methodists. Rather than originating the idea, Raikes simply made the idea more popular.

Unlike the broad education offered by the day schools, Sunday schools were set up solely for social training. Idle, uncontrollable, filthy and rude boys, who had been used to 'making hell' in the streets, were to be converted into well-disciplined, hard-working and polite young citizens who would be much less offensive to the middle classes (Sources A and C).

Many poor children at this time began work in the new factories at a very young age, because their parents much needed their earnings. Sunday was the only day when schooling would not interfere with their work. By holding schools on Sunday, it was also possible for adults who could not read or write to attend (Source D). There was also a very good supply of amateurs who were willing to help with the teaching on Sundays without pay. In some cases, a pupil–teacher ratio of as low as five to one was possible. This compared favourably with as many as eighty to one in some day schools.

The achievements of Sunday schools

In some places, Sunday schools formed **Sunday-school unions**. These unions provided the children with cut-price clothing, combs and free meals. The Society for the Establishment and Support of Sunday Schools in the Different Counties of England (established in 1785) organized local committees made up of representatives from the different churches. The society's rule was that the Bible should be taught thoroughly, and that the children should be taken to church.

Afraid that pupils might start to feel that manual labour was beneath them, it was decided to teach neither writing nor arithmetic in the Sunday schools. Yet, despite the narrowness of what they taught, Sunday schools were often greatly praised by their managers for making youngsters more civilized. These schools also did much to promote the idea of free education. This idea was taken up by the monitorial schools about a generation or so later.

SOURCE **B**

Robert Raikes, who wrote in the 'Gloucester Journal' in 1783: 'The misuse of Sunday appears, by the declaration of every criminal, to be their first step in the course of wickedness.'

SOURCE **A**

'That the Scholars be required to attend at their Schools with hands & face clean & hair cut short & combed, in the morning at nine o'clock & continue untill twelve & in the evening at two & remain till half past four. And if any of them be found guilty of lying, swearing, pilfering, talking in an indecent manner or otherwise misbehaving they be admonished, reproved & if after this they shall be judged incorrigible, they shall be discharged.'

◀ *Rules of the Madeley Sunday school, Shropshire, 1813.*

SOURCE C

'Farmers, and other inhabitants of the towns and villages, complain that they receive more injury to their property on the Sabbath than all the week besides: this, in a great measure, proceeds from the lawless state of the young who are allowed to run wild on that day, free from every restraint.

'To remedy this evil, properly qualified people and those that may have learnt to read are taught the Catechism and conducted to Church. By thus keeping their minds engaged, the day passes profitably. In those parishes where the plan has been adopted, we are assured that the behaviour of the children is greatly civilised.'

The benefits of Sunday schools, 'Gloucester Journal', 3 November 1783.

SOURCE D

'I had yesterday the pleasure of going with my Brother to Meole Brace. After Church we walked about & Miss Bather took me to visit a new house & school room lately built by W. Bather, it is a Sunday School & for the purpose of keeping up the knowledge of what has been learnt at the other schools in the parish when the boys are gone out to work & likewise to instruct any whose education has been neglected & who are too old for the charity schools. One married man, if not more, is a scholar there, who wishes to learn to read his Bible.'

A new Sunday school is opened at Meole Brace, Shropshire, 1812. (Extract from a diary of the time.)

SOURCE E

'Mr Raikes used always to come to school on Sundays and inquire what the children had learnt, and whether they had been "good boys". If there had been extra bad boys, then he would punish them himself.'

'How did he punish them?'

'The same way as boys were birched. An old chair was the birching stool or horse. The chair was laid on its two front legs, downward so, and then the young'un was put on so, kicking and swearing all the time.'

An old scholar's account of discipline in Raikes's Sunday school in Gloucester, 1800.

SOURCE F

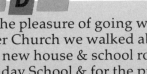

A list of people who gave money to the Sunday Schools in Bridgnorth, Shropshire, 1787.

EXERCISE

1 How do you think the owner of a Gloucester pin-factory would have felt about Robert Raikes's idea to set up a Sunday school in the town?

2 One of the visiting managers of a Sunday school notices that several of the teachers have started to teach the children to write. Do they pretend not to notice what is going on, or are they more likely to insist that writing is not to be taught?

3 If the teaching on Sunday was so limited, and was often of such poor quality, why didn't parents just send their children to a day school instead?

4 Sources A and E prove that punishments at Sunday schools in England in the nineteenth century were very harsh. Do you agree?

2.6 MONITORIAL SCHOOLS

EMPATHY

Many eighteenth-century schools had only about half a dozen children in them. Even the very largest usually had fewer than one hundred pupils. Such schools were run by one teacher, or a teacher and an assistant. As Britain's population grew in the early nineteenth century, schools of this size, taught in a single class, could not cope with the rapid rise in the number of children of school age.

Joseph Lancaster, the founder of the **British and Foreign School Society** (set up in 1807), and Dr Andrew Bell, who began the **National Society** (1811), came up with an inexpensive answer to the problem: the **monitorial system** (Source B). Bell had begun his schools in India, and this is why they were sometimes called **Madras schools**. the idea was that the teacher would train a small group of the oldest children at the beginning of each day, and these 'monitors' would then teach small groups of younger children. The teacher would all the while keep watch over the school from a platform at the front of the hall (Source A). In this way, schools of two or three hundred children could be run by a single teacher at very little cost, because the monitors cost next to nothing to employ.

In many ways, the monitorial school resembled a factory. The children were like the raw material. They would all be made into identical products, filled with the same information and ideas. Like a factory, the schoolroom was highly organized. The pupils sat in rows (Sources A and C) and were called out of their place only to go to their reading posts. Everything had to be done in a set way (Source D). The learning was done by reciting or chanting out aloud, learning by heart and copying on to a slate. There was very little, if any, genuine understanding.

SOURCE B

'It is not proposed that the children of the poor be educated in an expensive manner, or even taught to write and do arithmetic. There is a risk of elevating them from the drudgery of daily labour above their condition, and thereby making them discontented and unhappy in their lot. It may be enough to teach most children to read their Bible, and understand the doctrines of our Holy Religion.'

Andrew Bell, on the advantages of the monitorial system, 1807.

SOURCE A

The model Lancastrian school, Borough Road, London.

SOURCE C

Clapham School, London, 1810. This monitorial school was built to educate two hundred boys.

EMPATHY

Very few subjects were taught at monitorial schools, compared with the choice on offer today. There was no equipment to teach history, geography or science. Lessons were confined to spelling, writing, addition and subtraction. Kites and hoops, which were strung from the ceiling, were offered as rewards for the best pupils. Pupils who misbehaved were brought to the front and caned, as an example to the others.

Only children who were 'decently clothed, with clean heads, hands and faces', short hair, and, in the case of the Margate National School, carrying pocket handkerchiefs, were allowed into these schools. This clearly excluded the very poor, who had to settle for what were known as 'ragged schools'.

SOURCE D

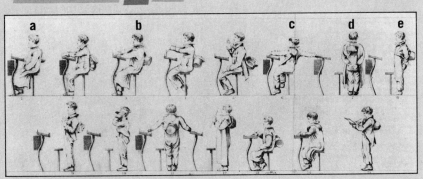

'Nine o'clock
School begins. The children, on entering, go to their desks, and the master reads a chapter from the Bible, the boys remaining perfectly quiet (a).

'Fifteen minutes past nine
The training of the monitors: the mass of the school writing on slates (b). Preparatory to writing, the general monitor of order would say 'Recover'; the boys bring their hands to the string of the slates – 'Slates shown up'. 'Lay down slates' . . . 'Clean slates'; the writing is rubbed out – 'Hands'; they cease rubbing the slate – 'Down'; they sit prepared for writing . . .

'Twelve o'clock
The school is dismissed. The commands for this are 'Sling'; each boy touches the slate sling with his left hand, and the lower end of his slate with his right hand. 'Slates'; each is lifted over the upper end of the desk and suspended (c). 'Hands down' – 'Look' – 'Turn' (d) – 'Out'; they jump out of the seats and stand. 'Front'; they face the monitor (e). 'Unsling'; they bring up the fingers of both hands to the strings which fasten their hats to the backs. 'Hats'; untie the strings and place the hats on the desks. 'Put on hats', 'Hands behind', 'Look' – they are then turned in the direction of the doors. 'Go'; led out quietly, or repeating tables.'

EXERCISE

1 Study Source B. Why was Bell so concerned about what was taught in these schools, and about the cost of it all?

2 Large numbers of children entered the new monitorial schools. Why, then, did some parents not see the benefits of these schools, and instead keep their children at home?

3 Nineteenth-century factories were full of adults as well as children. They had strict rules about work times and behaviour. In a noisy and stuffy atmosphere, the workers mass-produced goods for sale. How do you think children felt when they left a monitorial school and went to work in such a factory? Explain your answer.

4 How do you think the headteacher of a monitorial school would have reacted if a child from a poor family with dirty clothes and a runny nose had arrived one morning and said that their parents wanted them to go to school, so could they start straight away? Give reasons for your answer.

◀ *Guide for teachers in monitorial schools.*

2.7 SCHOOLS FOR THE MIDDLE CLASSES

From the last quarter of the eighteenth century, there are a huge number of advertisements in local newspapers for **private schools**. People had to pay to send their children to these schools, which meant that only middle-class families – not the poor – could afford them.

Private schools varied a great deal in the subjects they offered. Some taught practical subjects like writing, accounts and book-keeping. Others were more like 'finishing schools', teaching dancing, fencing and 'deportment' (or good posture). School fees and the quality of the education also varied widely. Some were day schools, while others took in boarders. Most of them, however, were single-sex schools.

SOURCE A

DANCING AND FENCING.

THE Friends of Mr. BOURLAY are respectfully informed, his ACADEMY, upon St. John's Hill, will re-open on MONDAY, the 21st Instant.

DANCING ACADEMY.

MR. LA FEUILLADE respectfully informs his Friends, and the Public in general, that his ACADEMY opens again on WEDNESDAY, the 30th Instant.

College Hill, Jan. 15th, 1805.

'Shrewsbury Chronicle', 18 January 1805.

SOURCE B

GRAMMAR SCHOOL, WEM.

WILL be Opened again on Monday the 25th of January, 1808.
Revd. F. SALT, Head Master.
TERMS.
Board (including the Latin and Greek Languages), 30 Guineas per Annum.
Entrance 2 Guineas. —— Washing 2 Guineas.
The other Branches of Education by the most approved Masters, on the usual Terms.

'Shrewsbury Chronicle', 8 January 1808.

SOURCE C

ADVERTISEMENTS.

MRS. GOATLY in Burgate, Canterbury, has lately open'd a School; and she Teaches therein to Draw for Working; likewise, to Paint upon Sattins, Silk and Holland, in a most beautiful manner, it being a very fashionable and diverting Work: Also, she sells Patterns for Gimp-work, Gowns, Coats and Habits, and all sorts of Work whatever.

'Kentish Post', 24–7 April 1728.

SOURCE E

Whitchurch, July 2, 1806.
EDUCATION.

MISS MARY JONES, respectfully informs her Friends and the Public, that her SCHOOL will Open on the 21st of JULY. YOUNG LADIES will be furnished with every convenient and comfortable Accommodation. Miss M. Jones begs Leave to return her sincere Thanks to her Friends for the Favours she has already experienced, and hopes by her Assiduity and Attention to the Morals and Improvement of her Pupils, to merit the Approbation of those Parents who will do her the Honour of intrusting their Children to her Care.
TERMS.

	£.	s.
Board and Education by the Year		
Entrance	17	17
Tea, if required	1	1
Writing, Arithmetic, French, Music, Drawing, and Dancing, by proper Masters, on the usual Terms.	2	2

'Shrewsbury Chronicle', 11 July 1806.

SOURCE D

AT Mr. Amoss's, a Baker, in St. George's, Canterbury, on Tuesday the 10th of January, will be Open'd (and Continued every Tuesday and Thursday) a DANCING SCHOOL; where all Young Gentlemen and Ladies will be Taught with the utmost Care and Diligence, by
ROBERT NEWHOUSE, Dancing-Master.

'Kentish Post', 28–31 December 1737.

SOURCE F

AT Mr. Lanes, over-against the Fountain Tavern in St. Margaret's, Canterbury, are Taught Writing, Arithmetick, and Merchants Accounts, with Exchanges from all Parts of Europe; Difcounts, Stocks, Securities, &c. neceffary for all Merchants: Alfo Book keeping for Shop-keepers, &c. after a Mercantile Manner. The Mafter may be fpoke with at the Coffee-Houfe every Wednefday and Saturday at Twelve o'Clock; and at any other time at his Lodgings above-mention'd. N. B. Gentlemen or Ladies may be Taught at their own Houfes, by their Humble Servant, JOHN ARY.

'Kentish Post', 19–23 December 1730.

SOURCE G

Board and Tuition.

THE ACADEMY at THE GREEN, on the Caftle Hill, BRIDGNORTH, will Open on the 27th of July, by the Rev. E.H. PAYNE, A. M. Chrift Church, Oxford, for the Reception of TWELVE YOUNG Gentlemen. Terms and Particulars may be known by perfonal Application, or by Letters Poft-paid.

N. B. French, Drawing, and Mufic, by approved Mafters.

'Shrewsbury Chronicle', 10 July 1807.

SOURCE H

BRIDGNORTH BOARDING-SCHOOL.

MISS WOODWARDS moft refpectfully inform their Friends and the Public, that their SCHOOL for the Education of a limited Number of PUPILS will re-open on MONDAY the 17th of JULY. They alfo take this Opportunity of expreffing their Gratitude to the Parents of thofe Young Ladies whofe Health and Education has been entrufted to their Care, affuring them and Others, who may place the fame Confidence in them, that no Exertions will ever be wanting which may promote their Health, Comfort, and Improvement; and every Pains will be taken to inftill into their unfolding Minds, thofe religious and virtuous Principles, which are the Bafis of prefent and future Happinefs. There are feveral Vacancies, a Half Boarder is wanting.

Applications, Poft-paid, will be attended to.

'Shrewsbury Chronicle', 27 June 1806.

SOURCE I

In the Great Room, up One Pair of Stairs, in the ROSE, Canterbury;

WRiting and Accounts, as alfo the Court Hand, Chancery Hand, and all the Law Hands, with their True Abbreviations taught to Clerks, (as true and in as fhort a time as by any Mafter in London,)

By J. Bartlett, who was bred a Clerk in the Court of King's Bench, Weftminfter.

N. B. Notwithftanding I Teach Abroad, I keep in my School as many Hours as other Mafters, and Teach my Scholars to Spell three Days in the Week; and will undertake to Teach any Servants, that cannot fpare time to come to School, to Write a good Legible Round Hand, by a fhort and eafy Method, only by Calling on me twice or thrice in the Week, for Half a Guinea.

Young Ladies Taught the Italian Hand, at their own Houfes, either by the Great or Quarter.

'Kentish Post', 19–22 January 1726.

ACTIVITY

Copy out the table below. Complete the table by filling in Sources A to I in the most suitable column.

	Schools offering . . .	
A classical training	*Vocational skills to boys*	*Training in social arts and graces*

QUESTIONS

1   What extra information about the running of private schools can we get from Sources A to I?

2   Is this new information reliable?

2.8 THE GROWTH OF PRIVATE SCHOOLING

CAUSATION

During the eighteenth century trade expanded and there was a large rise in numbers of merchants and tradespeople. Some business people began to get as wealthy as aristocrats. This growing middle class wanted to send its children to schools that were as good as the old-established grammar and public schools.

The public schools catered for the children of the aristocracy and were unwilling to open their doors to the offspring of the 'new rich'. In any case, they could not cope with the numbers. The grammar schools could cope, up to a point. However, the classical subjects they offered – Latin and Greek – were not thought useful by people who had made money in the business world. Also the management of the grammar schools was often in the hands of town corporations, which were unwilling to modernize the subjects taught.

Alongside these grammar schools, therefore, a whole range of **small private schools** were set up during the eighteenth century. We know this because of the large number of advertisements for these schools appearing in local newspapers. They offered subjects that were much more useful to the middle classes than what the grammar schools taught. And their smaller size, gentler discipline and more homely arrangements appealed to parents more than the larger size and harsher atmosphere of the grammar and public schools did.

Among the more useful subjects on offer in these new private schools were specialist skills such as surveying, book-keeping, merchants' accounting and shorthand. Others provided training in etiquette, dancing, fencing and deportment. French, the language of polite society, was taught by native speakers. Some men and women opened up private dancing and fencing establishments. One of these, Monsieur Bourlay of Shrewsbury, offered dancing so as to 'polish the Human Frame, with Grace, Ease and Elegance, so universally admired in the Beau Monde' and 'so requisite for genteel life'.

There was, it seems, an element of snobbery in this approach to education. By giving their children a chance to learn the 'social graces', middle-class parents hoped their sons and daughters would 'rise higher' in the social scale.

Boarding schools were more expensive than day schools. Boarders lived their whole lives at school during term time, and such schools provided more individual attention, usually having fewer pupils than day schools. Boarding establishments considered themselves superior to day schools – as their proprietors sometimes worked very hard to stress (Source A).

The curriculum at most boarding schools included English, arithmetic, geography, history, French and drawing. Other subjects might be painting, music, riding and fencing. Hard-working youngsters were promised a bright future at the universities, in the army or navy, in commerce or in professions that needed technical ability. Boys were often taught to write in **copperplate style** – handwriting elegant enough to be etched on copper and printed from for business purposes (Source C.) Girls' schooling was more geared to social and domestic skills such as

SOURCE A

'A Report having been circulated, that Miss HAWKINS admits DAY SCHOLARS, She takes the Liberty of contradicting it, and assures her Friends that she never means to deviate from her First Plan, and that her SCHOOL is OPEN ONLY for the Reception of BOARDERS.'

A notice in the 'Shrewsbury Chronicle', 16 November 1798.

SOURCE B

'R. TOMLINS, Writing-Master, impressed with Sentiments of the strongest Gratitude, returns his Thanks to the Inhabitants of this Town and Neighbour-hood for all Favors received, and most respectfully informs them, and the Public in general, that he has opened a WINE VAULT, at his House, on PRIDE-HILL, near the Butter-Cross, and has laid in a fresh Assortment of the very best Foreign Wines, French Brandy, Jamaica Rum, Hollands Geneva, British Brandy, Geneva, and all kinds of the best Cordials now used, which he intends to sell Genuine (as delivered to him) on the most reasonable Terms, for ready Money only. All Orders will be punctually executed, and gratefully acknowledged.

'N.B. The School will be carried on as usual (except Sewing) by R. TOMLINS, and proper Assistants.'

An advertisement placed by R. Tomlins in the 'Shrewsbury Chronicle', 19 November 1793.

dancing and embroidery. Sometimes the instruction given could not have been very good, because of the disruptions caused by the teachers having other jobs besides running a school (Source B).

Private schools were often family businesses. Mothers worked together with their daughters, and pairs of unmarried sisters commonly taught alongside each other. For example, in Shrewsbury during the early nineteenth century there could be found Jemima and Letitia Perry on Pride Hill, Eliza and Jane Pritchard in Castle Street, 'the Misses Puttrell' in Mardol, 'the Misses Wiseman' in Belmont and 'the Misses Field' in St Alkmond's Place. Some schools remained in the hands of one family for several generations.

A new development for students aged 16 and over in the eighteenth century was the growth of **academies**. These were intended for the children of **Nonconformists**. These people had been excluded from the universities of Oxford and Cambridge since the 1660s. Soon, however, academies became popular with Anglicans as well. This was partly because the teaching was often of a higher standard than that on offer in the universities. Another strength was that the curriculum was of more practical use, including scientific, commercial and business subjects, rather than simply the classics. It was also much cheaper for students to live at the academies than at the universities.

In summary, private schooling expanded because the increasingly large and prosperous middle classes believed that education held the key to social advance, either by gaining skills or through marriage into the nobility.

EXERCISE

1 Was the desire for social training all that is needed to explain the increase in the number of private schools?

2 Put the following causes and effects (results) into their proper order, giving a reason for each of your links.

Cause

dancing, deportment and embroidery were taught

the Industrial Revolution

the old-established public schools were full

Effect

a demand for a better-educated workforce

many private schools were built

improved marriage prospects

3 A teacher would lose his or her job if he or she had alcoholic drink in the classroom today. What reason might Mr Tomlins (Source B) have had for selling wines and spirits?

SOURCE C

A writing master's polished handwriting on his trade card, c. 1700.

2.9 THE GRAMMAR SCHOOLS: DECLINE AND CHANGE

CHANGE

By the end of the eighteenth century, the grammar schools generally were in a sorry state. In 1795 Lord Kenyon described them as 'empty walls without scholars'. This was partly because their income – based on old **endowments** (gifts of money or property) – was worth less and less, due to inflation. Another reason was that the subjects they taught were of little use to children who would have to go into trade when they left school. Even the law courts and the church had replaced Latin and Greek with English for their official records. Poor parents had long since decided that they would prefer to have their children working from them at home.

SOURCE A

Traditional speeches given in the Chapter House by scholars of the ancient King's School, Canterbury, 1845.

SOURCE C

The undersigned being desirous to consult the Inhabitants of Drayton as to the future application of the Funds of the

GRAMMAR SCHOOL,

BEG TO CONVENE A

PUBLIC MEETING

Of the Parishioners, to be held in the Grammar School,

ON THURSDAY MORNING NEXT, AUGUST 31ST,

AT ELEVEN O'CLOCK.

To take into consideration the propriety of making application to the proper quarter for authority to convert it into a

Commercial School,

And to obtain the requisite powers to make it as generally available as the Funds will permit.

THOMAS SLANEY, } Churchwardens.
EDMUND LLOYD, }

Market-Drayton, August 25th, 1848.

BENNION, PRINTER, DRAYTON.

A public notice from Market Drayton, Shropshire, 1848.

SOURCE B

A grammar school in ruin: Nixon's School, Oxford, c. 1890.

SOURCE D

'... that the said Master Teach the Grammar, commonly call'd King Henry Eighth Grammer.

'Before he admit any Scholar, the said Scholar be able to write compleatly, and to read perfectly Latin and English.

'... that the Master make choice of good Authors to read in the School, such as treat of moral Doctrine and Virtuous precepts.'

Rules of Biddenden Grammar School, Kent, 1675.

The grammar schools continued to empty, and many were forced to change their curriculum. In Shropshire, for example, at Halesowen, Shinfal and Wem there were no pupils studying Latin or Greek by the 1830s. Instead, subjects more useful for the world of work, such as writing and arithmetic, had been introduced. At Oswestry Grammar School, algebra, geometry and history were now taught. Grammar schools in the poorer countryside abandoned teaching the classics even earlier than the urban schools did.

The **Grammar Schools Act of 1840** came to recognize this situation by giving schools official permission to experiment with new subjects. Market Drayton Grammar School was forced to introduce more business subjects in 1848 (Source C). Some of the older schools, however, such as King's School, Canterbury (Source A), or schools under an able or energetic headteacher, such as Bradford Grammar School under Benjamin Butler (1728–84), survived without changing. But where a school was already struggling and could not change its regulations, the Charity Commissioners sometimes transferred its income to other local schools which taught only reading and writing (Source B).

SOURCE E

'WANTED: For the FREE-SCHOOL, at BIDDENDEN in KENT, A MASTER, being a Layman, to teach Latin, English, Writing, and Arithmetick.'

An advertisement in the 'Kentish Post', 20–23 March, 1765.

SOURCE F

1936	1986	
Reading	English	Office technology
Writing	Mathematics	Dance
Arithmetic	General studies	Geography
History	PE and games	Religious education
Geography	Art	English literature
Biology	Community service	Typing
Religious instruction	Human biology	Child development
Music	Integrated science	Computer studies
PE and games	Commerce	Home and food
Country dancing	French	studies
Sewing	History	
Domestic science	Fashion/Fabrics	

Subjects taught at a girls' school in Tonbridge, Kent, in 1936 and 1986.

EXERCISE

1 'Change in the grammar schools was sometimes held back, not by lack of enthusiasm, but by respect for the law.' Is there any evidence in the sources to support this statement?

2 Source A is dated 1845. Source B is dated *c.* 1890. Do these two sources prove that grammar-school education got worse between these years?

3 Look at Sources D and E.

a What changes were there in the curriculum at Biddenden Grammar School between 1675 and 1765?

b Do these changes mean that there was progress?

4 a What do you notice about the pace of educational change in the 1780s and the 1980s?

b Is there any similarity between the changes in question 3 and the changes which the school curriculum is undergoing today? (See Source F.)

2.10 EDUCATION FOR THE RICH

EVIDENCE

In the same way that rich and poor were not expected to socialize together, so their schools were also set apart. While the curriculum for the poor was limited to what would make them useful workers and obedient citizens, the schooling of rich youngsters was much more varied. Subjects for children of wealthy parents ranged from the classics to the sciences and also included training in the social behaviour of the ruling class.

There were three types of school for the rich: first, public schools – for boys only; secondly, seminaries, academies and boarding or day schools; and thirdly, private tutorials.

Leading **public schools** at this time were Eton (Sources A and B), King's School, Canterbury, Rugby, Shrewsbury, Westminster and Winchester. Despite the name 'public' schools, their very high fees and classical instruction in Greek, Latin and sometimes

SOURCE A

Eton College in the mid-nineteenth century.

SOURCE B

Eton boys in a wine cellar, nineteenth century.

SOURCE C

'Dr Arnold, the headmaster, 'gives out, after prayers in the morning, that no boy is to go down into the town. Wherefore East and Tom, for no earthly pleasure except that of doing what they are told not to do, start away, after second lesson, and making a short circuit through the fields, strike a back lane which leads into the town, go down it, and run plump upon one of the masters as they emerge into the High Street . . .

'He sends East and Tom up to the Doctor; who, on learning that they had been at prayers in the morning, flogs them soundly. They have each been flogged several times in the half-year for direct and wilful breaches of rules.'

An extract from the classic by Thomas Hughes, 'Tom Brown's Schooldays', 1857, about life at Rugby School.

SOURCE D

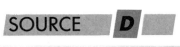

THE MISSES BEETLESTONE receive a limited number of Young Ladies to Board and Instruct, in the essentials of a sound and liberal Education, with accomplishments, assisted by efficient Masters.

The course of Instruction comprises, History, Literature, Geography, Grammar, Composition, Writing and Arithmetic, Delineation of Maps, Plain and Fancy Needlework.

Terms Per Annum.

Board with English £30 0 0
Under Ten years of 22 0 0
Daily Pupils per Quarter 1 5 0
Under Eight years 1 1 0
Music and Singing each 1 1 0
French and Drawing 1 1 0
Laundress 0 15 0

A select number of little Boys are also received, and instructed in the English, Latin, and French Languages, Terms as above. No allowance for temporary absence.

A Term's notice required previous to the removal of a Pupil.

Each Pupil to be provided with Sheets, Towels, Serviettes, Knife, Fork, Tea and Dessert Spoons.

References are kindly permitted to the Parents of Pupils who will gladly testify to the care manifested to promote the health and happiness of the Pupils.

Prospectus for a Shrewsbury ladies' boarding school, c. 1844.

Hebrew appealed only to the most wealthy. Many of these schools funded university scholarships at Oxford and Cambridge for their brightest pupils. Rules were severe, and punishments were brutal, floggings being very common (Source C). The public schools placed special emphasis on sports, and their prefect system gave older boys a chance to develop leadership qualities.

While many children of wealthy parents went to public schools, large numbers were sent to exclusive schools called **academies** or **seminaries**. Here they would learn French, the 'use of the globes' (geography), fencing and other skills. The emphasis was on learning 'refined' manners and the 'correct' social behaviour; pupils sometimes had to bring their own linen or silver cutlery.

Private tutorials took place in the homes of the aristocracy and the extremely wealthy (Source E). Brothers and sisters were educated in this way together, or teaching was one-to-one. The teachers who catered for this market rarely stated their fees in advertisements. Money was no object.

Having left one such school, a young gentleman (though not a young lady) might go on the **'Grand Tour'**. This meant a journey through Europe under the guidance of his tutor, intended to 'finish off' his education. In France the young man would improve his French and also have the chance to practise horse-riding and fencing. Later, by visiting Italy, he would be able to cultivate a taste for the fine arts and attend parties and balls. Visits to ancient classical sites in Greece and Italy were also included.

SOURCE E

A tutor teaches young ladies 'the use of the globes'.

EXERCISE

1 a Does Source A support the evidence in Source B about life at Eton College?

  b 'Because Source B is only a humorous cartoon, it is not as reliable as Source A.' Do you agree with this conclusion?

2 a What is there in Source B to make you suspect it is biased?

  b If there is any bias, does this mean that Source B is useless to the historian?

3 Source C is from a novel.

  a Does this make it automatically unreliable for historians?

  b Can the source still be useful?

4 'Source D gives historians a great deal of information about the Mansion House School, Shrewsbury. It also shows an accurate detailed picture of it.' Do you agree with this conclusion?

5 Which of the following statements about the education of girls can be supported by Sources D and E?

  a Girls' schools were small in size.

  b A good choice of subjects was taught in these schools.

  c Men taught in girls' schools.

3.1 BACKGROUND TO GOVERNMENT INVOLVEMENT

As already described, during the eighteenth century the government had not interfered in education. This was part of a general belief in *laissez-faire*, leaving people to provide for their families as they thought best and however they could. As far as education was concerned, the government was content with the work being done by the church and by individuals in providing a mixture of charity schools, Sunday schools, 'dame', 'common day' and private schools.

However, in the period after about 1780, people's lives were changing rapidly with the effects of the Industrial Revolution. Between 1750 and 1850 the population of Great Britain probably increased by almost two and half times (Source B). The traditional **domestic system** of producing goods by people working in their own homes could not cope with the new demand. Workers were needed to operate the new machines in the factories and mills. Better-educated clerks and craftspeople were also required. These major changes made it essential that the scope of education was widened to include the children of more ordinary men and women.

By this time, there were also increasing numbers of people who supported the idea of **national education**. They were not, however, united in their motives and beliefs. Some were **philanthropists**. These people were willing to give money for no other reason than the belief that it was right to do so. Others were **economists**, keen to maximize production and not to waste talent. Some economists thought it made good sense to educate the poor so that they could do a useful job in life and benefit the country. Still others were **social reformers** who wanted to give ordinary people more opportunities and a better life.

Parliament only came over very slowly to believe in popular education. As late as 1807, when **Samuel Whitbread** introduced a proposal to raise local money to support schools, his Bill was rejected by the House of Lords. There were two reasons for this opposition. First, it was felt that, if the poor were educated, they would be in a position to read anti-government propaganda, and would become unhappy about their lowly position in society (Source A).

Philanthropists, economists and social reformers.

SOURCE A

'Giving education to the labouring classes of the poor, would be harmful to their morals and happiness; it would lead them to despise their lot in life, instead of making them good servants in agriculture and other work to which their rank in society had destined them. It would enable them to read vicious books, and publications against Christianity; it would make them insolent to their superiors. Besides, if the Bill were to pass into law, it would burden the country with a most enormous and incalculable expense.'

Debate on Samuel Whitbread's Bill, 1807.

A second criticism, voiced by the bishops, was that the scheme would remove the schools from the control of the Church of England. Joseph Lancaster, a Quaker, founder of the **British and Foreign School Society**, blamed the rivalry between the different Christian churches for the delays in developing a system of national education.

By the 1830s, stronger doubts were expressed about the fairness of the *laissez-faire* principle generally. To some, it was only acceptable if each person had the same power to do as they wished. Otherwise, giving people the freedom to do as they wished could mean giving freedom to the strong to exploit the weak. Cheating shopkeepers could water down milk and ale; and employers could make their employees work long hours in poor conditions, sacking any who did not fall into line.

These opinions were more and more widely shared. During the nineteenth century, the government became increasingly involved in education, until eventually it took over complete responsibility for it. The philosopher T. H. Green argued that it was the positive duty of the state to make sure that all its citizens could use their talents for the common good. He called this idea **positive freedom**. It meant the government intervening to deal with mass urban poverty, cholera epidemics, ignorance and lack of self-respect.

SOURCE **B**

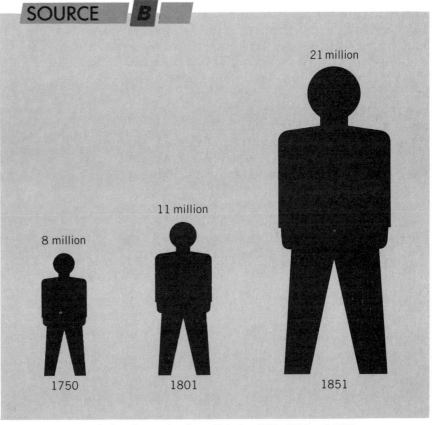

21 million

11 million

8 million

1750   1801   1851

Approximate population figures for Great Britain: 1750, 1801 and 1851.

3.2 STATE INTERVENTION IN EDUCATION: FIRST STEPS

CHANGE

The government's first tentative step towards intervention in education was in 1833, when the **Treasury** granted £20,000 to the **British and Foreign School Society**, and to the **National Society** (see Unit 2.6) for building schools.

The conditions of this Treasury grant (Source A) were that no money would be paid until half the estimated cost of building a school had already been raised by a local collection. The grant was to be distributed by the two societies themselves, and they were responsible for maintaining the schools. The payment was increased in later years. By 1846 it amounted to £100,000, and by 1859 to £836,920. Although the amount was small, the grant was an important new step. It was proof of a major change of direction in government thinking – almost a revolutionary change. But it attracted little attention at the time.

That same year, 1833, the **Factory Act** made it illegal to employ children under 9 years old in most textile mills, and reduced the working day of older children. The **freeing of slaves** within the British Empire, and the compensation of their owners out of taxpayers' money, was another example that year of the government taking positive measures to improve the well-being of a minority.

Arguments for and against the change

For many years, the idea had been growing that England was in urgent need of schooling for all, and that only a **state system**, organized and financed by the government, could secure it. Writers such as the poet Coleridge (a Tory), Thomas Carlyle (a radical) and Charles Dickens shared this view. They felt that the state should see to it that all children received some minimum level of schooling, that the state should be willing to help pay for it, and that it should supervise the standard of teaching.

These ideas were not, however, shared by all. Many people were suspicious of what they saw as the government overstepping the mark, and trespassing into an area of individual freedom. And even the keenest supporters of state education were not looking for much more than a way of bringing out the best in each existing social rank; they did not think of schools as a way to reduce social inequalities.

SOURCE A

'That a Sum, not exceeding £20,000, be granted by His Majesty, to be issued in aid of Private Subscriptions for the Erection of School Houses, for the Education of the Children of the Poorer Classes in Great Britain, to the 31st day of March 1834; and that the said sum be issued and paid without any fee or other deduction whatsoever.'

The Government provides a grant towards education in the Revenue Act, 1833.

SOURCE B

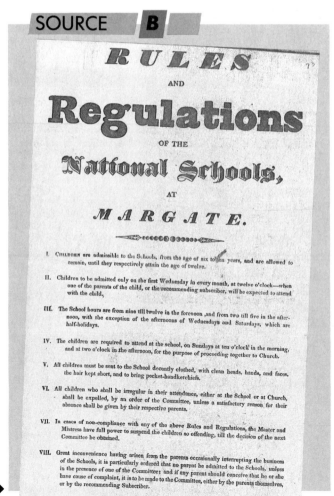

Rules and regulations of the National Schools at Margate. ▶

SOURCE C

'For a very small expense, the public can facilitate, can encourage and can even impose upon almost the whole body of the people, the necessity of acquiring those most essential parts of education.'

Adam Smith, 'The Wealth of Nations', 1776.

SOURCE D

'A nation under a well-regulated government should permit none to remain uninstructed. It is monarchical and aristocratic government only that requires ignorance for its support.'

Thomas Paine, 'The Rights of Man', 1792.

SOURCE E

'Government will not fail to employ education to strengthen its hand and perpetuate its institutions.'

William Godwin, 'Enquiry Concerning Political Justice', 1793. Godwin was strongly against state interference in education, even in a limited form.

SOURCE F

'Education is only government acting by means of a domestic magistrate. The less parents are able to discharge this duty, the more necessary it is for the government to fulfil it.'

*Jeremy Bentham, 'Principles of Penal Law', 1802. Bentham believed in the philosophy of **utilitarianism** (or 'usefulness'). He always asked the question, 'What use is an idea or an institution such as a university or a grammar school? Does it bring happiness to most people?' Only if it did could the idea or institution be justified.*

SOURCE G

'What! Educating one of the children of the shirking slip-shod – I will do no such thing. But I have other and most powerful objections, to *any plan* of "*national education*", which must of necessity create a new and most terrific control in the hands of the government. I am further of opinion and I know it to be true, indeed, that such a thing must be most injurious, not only to the morals but to the liberties of the country.'

William Cobbett, 'The Political Register', 21 September 1833.

EXERCISE

1 There had been discussion about a national system of education in England as far back as the 1630s.

   a What factors delayed this change in the period before 1833?

   b What other factors brought it about in 1833?

2 Thomas Paine (Source D) and William Cobbett (Source G) were both radicals, who worked to make changes to how the country was run. Is Thomas Paine's view in 1792 similar to or different from William Cobbett's in 1833?

3 The government's decision to make a grant for education in 1833 seems to us today to have been a great change. Explain why this was thought of as nothing very special at the time.

3.3 FURTHER STATE INTERVENTION IN EDUCATION

A **Committee of the Privy Council** was set up in 1839 to manage the new annual education grant. The committee remained in existence until 1856, when it was reorganized to become the **Education Department**. Its first Secretary, **Dr Kay-Shuttleworth**, found that throughout the country schools were poorly equipped and insanitary. Source A is an example of reports of the time.

To help do something about these poor conditions, the committee soon began to offer plans on school buildings to the two main education societies.

Inspectors and 'pupil-teachers'

The committee also appointed two **Schools Inspectors**: one for Church of England schools, and one for schools run by the British and Foreign Society. Their duties included visiting grant-aided schools to check that money was being properly spent, that discipline was good and that suitable methods of teaching were being used. In the view of these early Schools Inspectors, the main point of elementary education was to control the thoughts and habits of the working poor (see Source B).

The inspectors' job was to recommend improvements and, significantly, *to give encouragement* to the local school committees. As Kay-Shuttleworth stressed, they were not 'a means of exercising control, but of affording assistance'. Later, as we shall see, with the 'Revised Code', this good relationship came under strain.

By 1849 there were nineteen inspectors. Unless schools received a favourable report from them, they had their grant reduced or taken away altogether. The main aim of this system was to get the best possible value for money.

Inspectors also came to be appointed to investigate **factory schools**. The 1833 Factory Act had laid down that factory children were to have two hours' schooling a day, enforceable by inspectors. With the new **1844 Factory Act**, children between 8 and 13 who worked in factories had to spend either three full days or six half-days at school. These children, 'dirty and labour-soiled, in ragged and scanty clothes, with heavy eyes and worn faces' (inspectors' minutes, 1844), came to be known as '**half-timers**'.

With more children to teach, more teachers were urgently needed. In an effort to help provide more, and better-qualified, teachers, Kay-Shuttleworth introduced a **pupil-teacher system** in 1846. Each pupil-teacher had to be at least 13 years old and competent in reading, writing and arithmetic (the three Rs), as well as elementary geography, religious instruction and (for girls) sewing and knitting. They were also supposed to be able to teach a junior class. After serving their time, the pupil-teachers would then go on to a training college, or 'normal school', supported by grants from the Privy Council committee.

SOURCE **A**

'The schools were, for the most part, dirty and ill-ventilated. A rudely constructed desk for the master occupied one corner; forms and desks for the children were ranged along the walls, and from side to side. In many, silence was only maintained for a few minutes at a time by loud exclamations and threats; in one, a deserted chapel, half the space was occupied with hay piled up to the roof.'

The state of elementary education reported to the Committee of the Privy Council on Education, 1839–40.

SOURCE **B**

'No plan of education ought to be encouraged in which intellectual instruction is not subordinate to the regulation of the thoughts and habits of the children by the doctrines and precepts of revealed religion.'

Report of Schools Inspectors, 4 July 1840.

SOURCE **C**

Sir James Kay-Shuttleworth, 1804–77, 'founder of the English system of popular education'.

Biography of Dr James Kay-Shuttleworth, 1804–77.

There were three phases to Dr Kay-Shuttleworth's career, covering the fields of (1) medicine, (2) poverty and (3) education. There was a natural progression from one to the other.

1804 — Born James Phillips Kay at Rochdale, Lancs.

Phase (1): Medicine

1824 — Began studying medicine at Edinburgh University; elected senior president of Royal Medical Society; assisted during a typhus outbreak as a student.

1827 — Graduated MD with expertise on asphyxia; settled in Manchester to practise as a doctor.

Phase (2): Poverty

c.1830 — Became a Medical Officer in a poor, crowded area of Manchester.

1832 — Published findings in a pamphlet: *The Moral and Physical Condition of the Working Classes Employed in the Cotton Manufacture in Manchester*; it led to improvements in sanitation and education. Witnessed and assisted in great cholera outbreak.

1835 — Appointed Poor Law Assistant Commissioner for Norfolk and Suffolk, and later for London area. From these experiences, he concluded that 'education was one of the most efficient antidotes to hereditary pauperism.'

Phase (3): Education

In the next few years, he did experiments at an overcrowded workhouse school in Norwood, south London. When teachers were ill, deputies stood in as 'pupil-teachers'. They were paid a small salary, clothed in special uniforms, and had separate sleeping cubicles. He tried to set up a state teacher-training college but failed.

1839–40 — He set up a training college in Battersea, which he continued to run until he could no longer afford the expense (1842). The first students were eight (later twenty-four) pupil-teachers from Norwood School of Industry. As well as lessons, physical training, gardening and prayers took place. Meals were frugal.

1839 — Appointed Secretary of Privy Council Committee for Education. Visited Holland, France, Prussia and Switzerland, which had all established state systems of education.

1840 — Introduced system of school inspection, and issued instructions to Schools Inspectors.

1842 — Married, taking name of Kay-Shuttleworth.

1849 — Overwork forced his resignation from Privy Council Committee; made a baronet: Sir James Kay-Shuttleworth.

1877 — Died in London.

SOURCE D

Standard I

Reading — Narrative in monosyllables
A short paragraph from an elementary reading book used in the school

Writing — Form on blackboard or slate, from dictation, letters capital and small manuscript

Arithmetic — Form on blackboard or slat, form dictation, figures up to 20; name at sight figures up to 20; add and subtract figures up to 10, orally, and from examples on blackboard

Standard VI

Reading — A short ordinary paragraph in a newspaper, or other modern narrative

Writing — Another short ordinary paragraph in a newspaper, or other modern narrative, slowly dictated once by a few words at a time

Arithmetic — A sum in practice or bills of parcels

Top and bottom Standards from the 'Revised Code', 1862.

3.3

The 'Revised Code' and later developments

After fighting an expensive war in the Crimea, the British government wanted to save money. Some people felt that the education grant was not being well spent. In 1858 the **Newcastle Commission** was set up 'To inquire into the present state of Popular Education in England, and to consider and report what Measures, if any, are required for the extension of sound and cheap elementary instruction to all classes of the people'.

The commission's findings were published as the **Newcastle Report** in 1861. The report said:

- The teaching in public elementary schools was not geared to the needs of the children. It was often 'too ambitious and too superficial', and aimed more at the older children.
- Private schools were 'inferior as schools of the poor', and were ill-suited to giving them a useful education.
- Only about 20 per cent of children leaving public elementary schools at 12 years old were sufficiently educated.
- Although the teachers were better than before the pupil-teacher system began, still 'a large proportion of the children' were not satisfactorily taught the basic three Rs.

The report suggested that, in future, a school's education grant should depend upon its pupils reaching a good enough standard under examination. This scheme, introduced by the new vice-president of the Committee of the Privy Council on Education, **Robert Lowe**, as part of the **'Revised Code'** of 1862, became known as **payment by results**.

To obtain the full grant, it was essential for teachers to make sure that pupils attended school regularly, in order that they could progress through the six '**standards**' (see Source D). Worries about getting pupils through these standards led to schools teaching just what was needed for the exam. Learning took place parrot fashion, with little understanding. Another harmful effect was that the previous good relationship between teachers and Schools Inspectors, which Dr Kay-Shuttleworth had aimed at, was undermined. Understandably, Kay-Shuttleworth opposed the system from his retirement. The term 'standard' lingered, even when the system ended, and it is still used instead of 'form' in the USA today.

The system of payment by results seemed to many people an efficient way of improving education standards. However, not everyone thought that the curriculum of every school should be strictly practical. The **Clarendon Report (1864)** approved of the introduction of natural science into the curriculum. But, based on studying the industrial success of France and Germany, it concluded that the only way to produce leaders was through the mainly classical curriculum of the public schools. 'Great statesmen and great financiers at the head of the government rise out of a classical education,' the report said.

As more people gained the right to vote, the government saw the need to educate people so they would use it wisely. The widening of **voting rights** to include the middle classes in 1832

Biography of Robert Lowe, 1811–92.

1811
Born at Bingham, Notts. Educated at Winchester and University College, Oxford.

1835
Studied law at Lincoln's Inn.

1842
Called to the bar at that Inn, but then practised in Australia.

1843–50
Became a member of the legislative council for New South Wales, was famous for his speeches on education.

1846
Set up a national board of education in Australia.

1850
Became a journalist on *The Times*.

1852
Entered the House of Commons as MP for Kidderminster, and served until 1859.

1852–5
Was joint secretary of the Board of Control in Lord Aberdeen's government and (from 1855) a Privy Councillor.

1855–8
Appointed vice-president of the Board of Trade and Paymaster-general in Palmerston's government.

1859
Elected MP for Calne, Wilts.

1859–64
Made vice-president of the Committee of the Privy Council on Education, introducing the system of 'payment by results' in the 'Revised Code' of 1862.

1864
Resigned.

1868
Appointed Chancellor of the Exchequer under Gladstone.

1873–4
Home Secretary.

1880
Became First Viscount Sherbrooke.

1892
Died.

SOURCE **E**

Robert Lowe, 1811–92, who introduced the 'payment by results' system.

SOURCE **F**

John Stuart Mill, 1806–73, who argued that education was a matter for the individual parent, and not for the government.

was therefore followed by the Treasury grant to education of 1833. In the same way, the extension of the franchise to include working-class men in towns in 1867 was soon followed by the 1870 Education Act. As Robert Lowe commented at the time this **1867 Second Reform Act** was passed: 'We must compel our future masters to learn their letters.' There was widespread worry that an illiterate electorate could easily absorb revolutionary views without being able to question them.

Meanwhile, the **Taunton Commission** looked into **secondary education**. In 1868 it reported that girls were being taught social graces instead of basic skills. **The Girls' Public Day Schools Trust** (1872) founded new academic grammar schools to help improve this situation.

Increased pressure for the government to do more for education came from the Birmingham-based **National Education League** (established in 1869). Its president, the Nonconformist **Joseph Chamberlain**, campaigned for compulsory free education for all, and without teaching the beliefs of any particular religious group. Such education, he said, should be paid for from the rates, and governed by locally elected School Boards. Under Chamberlain's proposals, there was also to be a halt to the programme of building any more church schools. The league helped bring about the **1870 Education Act**, though Chamberlain's ambitions to make education free and compulsory were not fulfilled until later.

Slow progress
Why did the extension of a state system of education make such slow progress? There were three main problems affecting government educational activity.

One reason for the slow progress was the difficulty in overcoming the still strong *laissez-faire* spirit. Many people continued to believe that anything the government did beyond keeping order at home and defending the country during war took away individuals' freedom. Education was seen by many government ministers as a matter for the individual parent alone. This opinion was strongly argued by the philosopher **John Stuart Mill**, who had been educated by his father and boasted of being able to cope with ancient Greek at 5 years old.

A second difficulty, until the 1867 Second Reform Act made the extension of education urgent, was that the upper and middle classes were worried that educating the masses would upset the social system. Educated workers, it was believed, would become discontented. They would want a better life for themselves, and there would be a shortage of servants as a result.

Most seriously of all, **sectarianism** – bitter arguments between the Anglicans and the Nonconformists – held up progress. The Nonconformists wanted undenominational Bible-reading, rather than 'indoctrination' in the beliefs of the Church of England; they were also strongly opposed to financing church schools from the rates. The Church of England, for its part, wanted to teach children its own catechism, and to have its own inspectors.

3.4 THE 1870 EDUCATION ACT

CAUSATION

In 1801 the population of England and Wales was 9 million. In the next half a century or so it doubled. In fact, in the industrial towns and cities it had risen even faster than this (see Source A). There were now too many children for the British and National Societies, together with private charity, to cope with (see Source B).

The government had two worries. First, having large numbers of untaught children left roaming the streets was a bad waste of talent. A literate and skilled workforce was much needed in British industry, which was now losing ground to its rivals in Germany and the USA. Secondly, the government was worried that if these children were left untaught they would turn to crime. Workmen in the towns were allowed to vote for the first time in 1867, and this increased the pressure to build more schools to train the young to use their vote wisely when they became adults. The following year, 1868, **William Gladstone** and the **Whig** (or **Liberal**) **Party** won the general election. The new government listened to the Manchester Education Aid Society (founded in 1864) and the Birmingham Education League, which were pushing for compulsory education for all. It agreed that education could no longer be a voluntary activity as it had been under the *laissez-faire* Conservative governments. The state had to take a serious interest and take positive action. The aim of the Education Bill, which W. E. Forster introduced into Parliament in 1870, was to ensure that there was a school for elementary education within reach of every home in England.

The Education Act was passed that same year. It called for a census to be made of elementary school places in each parish. Where a local voluntary school already existed, nothing more was to be done. If there was no school, the parish was given six months to provide one. If it failed to do so, as often happened, a local **Board of Education** (School Board) had to be set up, with the task of raising a rate, buying land and building a school. Such schools would fill the gaps in the existing system.

A compromise was reached over **teaching religion**. Methodist, Baptist and other Nonconformist families would in future feel at ease in sending their children to Church of England schools. This was because of a '**conscience clause**' which excused them from Scripture lessons.

The boards could, if they wished, make it compulsory for their 5- to 11-year-olds to go to school by passing a local by-law, and by paying the fees of the poorest children.

SOURCE B

'I will now ask: What is it that we have not? Only two-fifths of the children of the working classes between the ages of 6 and 10 years are on the registers of the government schools, and only one-third of those between the ages of 10 and 12.

'We must not delay. Upon the speedy provision of elementary education depends our industrial prosperity. It is of no use trying to give technical teaching to our artisans without elementary education. If we leave our workfolk any longer unskilled, they will become over-matched in the competition of the world.'

W. E. Forster's speech introducing the Education Bill, 17 February 1870.

SOURCE C

'I suppose it will be absolutely necessary to educate our masters. From the moment you entrust the masses with power, their education becomes an imperative necessity. You have placed the government of this country in the hands of the masses and you must therefore give them an education.'

Speech made by Robert Lowe, vice-president of the Education Department, at the time of the Second Reform Act, 1867.

SOURCE A

	1750 estimate	1801	1841
Birmingham	30,000	71,000	202,000
Leeds	14,000	53,000	152,000
Liverpool	35,000	82,000	299,000
Manchester	45,000	75,000	252,000

◀ *Population figures for four English industrial cities, 1750, 1801 and 1841.*

There were some things that the 1870 Act did not change, however. The Act did not make it free for all children to go to school. Nor did it make school compulsory for all children.

SOURCE D

THE THREE R'S; OR, BETTER LATE THAN NEVER.

RIGHT HON. W. E. FORSTER (CHAIRMAN OF BOARD). "WELL, MY LITTLE PEOPLE, WE HAVE BEEN GRAVELY AND EARNESTLY CONSIDERING WHETHER YOU MAY LEARN TO READ. I AM HAPPY TO TELL YOU THAT, SUBJECT TO A VARIETY OF RESTRICTIONS, CONSCIENCE CLAUSES, AND THE CONSENT OF YOUR VESTRIES—*YOU MAY!*"

A cartoon from 'Punch', 26 March 1870.

SOURCE E

THE EDUCATION PROBLEM.

MASTER FORSTER. "PLEASE, M'M, I'VE DONE IT, M'M!"
SCHOOLMISTRESS (BRITANNIA). "AND *HOW* HAVE YOU DONE IT, WILLIAM?"
MASTER FORSTER. "PLEASE, M'M, I'VE REDUCED ALL THE FRACTIONS TO THE LOWEST COMMON DENOMINATION."
SCHOOLMISTRESS. "GOOD BOY! *GO UP!*"

[*The Good Boy enters the Cabinet.*

◀ *How the 'education problem' was solved 'Punch', 16 July 1870.*

EXERCISE

1 There was a need to educate those who had just been given the vote (Source C). Is this enough to explain the passing of the 1870 Education Act?

2 Are the following factors causes of the 1870 Education Act? In each case, give reasons for your answer.

   a More and more political cartoons were appearing in magazines.
   b Germany was experiencing an industrial revolution.
   c The population of English industrial towns had grown very rapidly.
   d A Whig government had been elected in 1868.
   e *Laissez-faire* ideas were becoming unpopular.

3 Consider only the factors you thought were causes of the 1870 Education Act in your answer to question 2. Do you think all these factors are equally important, or was one more important than the others? Give reasons for your answer.

4 There had been Whig governments before this time; and France, for example, had industrialized in the 1830s. Why, then, did mass elementary education not come about in England before 1870?

3.5 THE SCHOOL BOARD ERA, 1870–1901

The **School Boards** have often been seen as the earliest democratically elected local education authorities. They weakened the previous dominance of the squire and clergyman in the community. Their membership was unusual in sometimes including working men; and they also provided a unique opportunity for a few women to have a say in public life. All were now brought face to face with the realities of educating the poor: inadequate school buildings, and parents who preferred ignorance to education.

Elections to the new boards were often keenly contested. Once a committee was formed, one of the first actions of the School Board was to conduct a survey of the number of children in their district and estimate what schools needed to be provided. They then had the power to raise a **rate** (a local tax on land and building values). In some of the large towns, such as Birmingham and Liverpool, this rate could be as low as 1d in the £ (half a new penny in the pound) or even less; but in more sparsely populated areas, like Devon and Cornwall, it had to be as much as 6d in the £ (two and a half new pence in the pound).

The building of new schools began quickly in some areas. In London, the first **board school** was opened in 1873. The London board was the largest and most powerful in the country, and provided a model for others to follow. Among its members were the scientist T. H. Huxley, Elizabeth Garrett Anderson (one of the first women doctors) and the stationer W. H. Smith. Within two years, there were almost one hundred board schools in the capital. Whilst many boards in the industrial towns were large, progressive and energetic, in rural areas the board might be dominated by local farmers, whose main concern was often financial rather than educational – that is, to keep the rates as low as possible.

The most striking difference between the board school and the earlier monitorial school was its architecture. From the outside, it looked like a church (see Unit 3.6, Source B). Inside, instead of one big hall, it was divided into classes (Unit 3.6, Source C), each

SOURCE A

◀ *Children lining up to pay their weekly pennies.*

SOURCE B

SCHOOL BOARD AND WASHING:
OR, NO SOFT SOAP!

YOU DIRTY BOY!

The dirty School Board 'brat', 'Punch', 26 November 1881. In London the School Board gained a reputation for enrolling ragged, dirty children.

with a qualified assistant, and superintended by a headteacher who was largely an administrator.

The School Boards kept in touch with each other, often through the *School Board Chronicle*. They came to extend the scope of education far beyond what had been intended in the 1870 Act. The teaching of science, geography, English history, drawing and physical education was introduced alongside the three Rs. The larger boards also tried secondary education, and a few started to teach blind, deaf, epileptic and mentally handicapped children. Because they were financed from a rate that all property owners had to pay, board schools were able to buy better equipment than the earlier schools had. Also, their higher rates of pay attracted better qualified teachers.

In their earliest years, the School Boards in the major towns were unable to supply enough pupil-places. But many still passed by-laws making attendance compulsory for all 5- to 13-year-olds. They appointed officers known as '**board school men**' to round up children who were unwilling to come to school (see Unit 3.6, Source D).

A few towns also set up '**truant schools**' and '**industrial schools**' to take in the most difficult cases – 'incorrigible truants', 'children of a still more hardened class' and 'neglected children', all of whom would be given unpleasant tasks, like picking oakum. The boards would sometimes pay the fees of such deprived children, until 1891, when all children were given the right to be educated free of·charge. Until this time it had been usual for children to pay pennies (see Source A).

In spite of all this activity, however, some parents still kept their children at home, believing that the teachers were using them to do jobs on the cheap for them at school. Others, as quickly as possible at twelve o'clock or half-past four, collected their children so they could carry fruit and fish, run errands or work in their shops. Assaults on teachers by parents, for washing or cutting their children's hair, for example, were common.

Sandon's Act 1876 established that parents had a duty to see that their children received an education. To help them to put this idea into practice, the Act made it illegal to employ any child under 10 years old. At the same time, **School Attendance Committees** were forced upon any area without a School Board. In 1880 the **Mundella Act** made school attendance compulsory for children from 5 to 10 years of age. The leaving age was raised to 11 in 1893, and to 12 in 1899. Parents who failed to send their children to school were liable to be fined 2s 6d (12½p) for the first offence, and 5s 0d (25p) thereafter. There were very few convictions, because magistrates were reluctant to impose the penalty even when the evidence was overwhelming. The threat of such fines was therefore ineffective – parents knew they might escape the fine, and in any case working children's earnings provided more than enough to pay for a fine if it was imposed.

During the next twenty years, many School Boards took over bankrupted existing schools, whose managers were only too willing to pass on responsibility for them.

3.6 THE BOARD SCHOOLS

EVIDENCE

SOURCE A

'Look at those big isolated clumps of buildings rising above the slates, like brick islands in a lead coloured sea.'

'The Board Schools.'

'Lighthouses, my boy! Beacons of the future! Capsules, with hundreds of bright little seeds in each, out of which will spring the wiser, better England of the future.'

A conversation between Sherlock Holmes and Dr Watson about the London Board Schools, from Sir Arthur Conan Doyle's 'The Naval Treaty', c. 1890.

SOURCE B

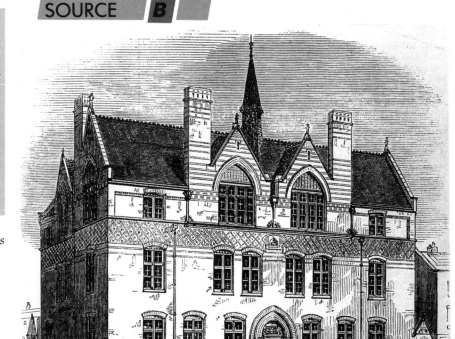

▶ *One of the earliest board schools in the New Kent Road, London. A central hall was surrounded by classrooms separated by partitions. Infants were on the ground floor, girls on the first floor and boys on the second.*

SOURCE C

The interior of a London board school. A class of forty on one side of an open partition is shown next to another class of fifty.

SOURCE D

The 'board school man' rounds up malingerers at night in London, 1871.

EXERCISE

1 Does the author of Source A approve of board schools? Explain your answer.

2 Do you think the school shown in Source B is the same as the school shown in Source C? Give reasons for your answer.

3 'The English board schools were run with a military-style precision and discipline.' On the basis of the sources here, do you think this statement is true? Give reasons for your answer.

4 Is Source E a primary or a secondary source? Explain your answer.

5 Is it fair to suggest, on the basis of the sources here, that the country must have thought education was very important in the years after 1870? Explain your answer.

6 Which of these sources do you think a historian studying the board schools would find most useful? Give reasons for your answer.

SOURCE E

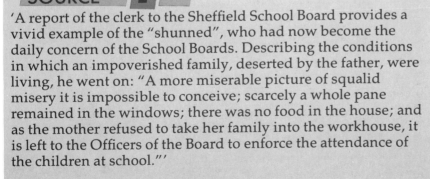

'A report of the clerk to the Sheffield School Board provides a vivid example of the "shunned", who had now become the daily concern of the School Boards. Describing the conditions in which an impoverished family, deserted by the father, were living, he went on: "A more miserable picture of squalid misery it is impossible to conceive; scarcely a whole pane remained in the windows; there was no food in the house; and as the mother refused to take her family into the workhouse, it is left to the Officers of the Board to enforce the attendance of the children at school."'

Description of the living conditions of a Sheffield Board School child, c.1880.

3.7 RIVALRY BETWEEN CHURCH AND BOARD SCHOOLS

EMPATHY

" OBSTRUCTIVES."

Mr. Punch (*to* Bull A I). "YES, IT'S ALL VERY WELL TO SAY, 'GO TO SCHOOL!' HOW ARE THEY TO GO TO SCHOOL WITH THOSE PEOPLE QUARRELLING IN THE DOORWAY? WHY DON'T YOU MAKE 'EM 'MOVE ON'?"

As we have seen, the 1870 Education Act allowed two kinds of elementary school. Where the voluntary **church schools** were coping well, they were allowed to continue alongside the new 'gap-filling' **board schools**. The existence of these two types of school side by side was called the '**dual system**'.

A cartoon from 'Punch', 2 July 1870. A group of clergymen argue, with a dean in the centre, blocking the school door. Meanwhile, Mr Punch explains to the policeman that it is pointless trying to make children go to school when they can't get in.

Opposition

The dual system of church schools and board schools was not a peaceful partnership. The Church of England was very critical of the board schools. It distrusted and feared the control that ratepayers would wish to have over the running of these schools (Source A). The opposition was led by bishops. The Bishop of Hereford urged the ratepayers to vote against a board, unless they wanted their rates raised and their wages reduced. Wealthy Tory farmers joined the side of the clergy. They sometimes took their tenants to the election by force, making them vote against the setting up of a School Board; in other cases, tenants were evicted if they voted for a School Board.

EMPATHY

A major reason for the church's opposition was over the 'undenominational' religious teaching laid down in the 1870 Act, together with the '**Cowper-Temple clause**', which allowed parents to withdraw their children from Scripture. Most School Boards were happy that religious instruction should be made up of plain Bible-reading and moral instruction, without teaching any particular kind of Christianity. But the Bishop of Ely commented that he 'would rather see Mahometanism (Islam) taught in the country than have that undogmatic Christianity.' Church officials continued to appoint only committed Church of England men and women as teachers. And these teachers were told that it was their duty to explain to the children why they should be Anglicans, rather than Catholics, Methodists, Quakers or other Nonconformists.

Meanwhile, the **1888 Cross Commission** revealed that the boards at Birmingham, St Neots and Padstow had gone so far as to give no religious instruction whatever.

The dual system of voluntary and board schools lasted, in this form, for just over thirty years. One of its weaknesses was that, although board schools in the towns might be well off, countryside schools were often few and far between, especially where there was one large landowning farmer. In 1902 the countryside provision was levelled up to a position more equal to that of the towns. The **Education Act 1902** replaced the School Boards with **Local Education Authorities** (LEAs), which controlled town and country parishes alike within their areas.

EXERCISE

1 How do you think a Methodist potter living in North Staffordshire would feel about settling his differences with the Church of England quickly and peacefully and building well-equipped schools together?

2 Consider the position of the chairman of a managing committee at a small Church of England school. A large board school has just been built in the town, and he is worried that his pupils might leave for the board school. Which of the following policies would he advise his committee to follow?
  a Bring down their fees, in line with those of the board school.
  b Broaden the curriculum; that is, introduce more subjects into the school.
  c Stop all punishments at the school.
  d A combination of the above policies.
  You will need to consider the advantages and disadvantages of each policy. Give reasons for your eventual choice.

3 How do you think a member of the Church of England and a Nonconformist would each react on first hearing about each of these events:
  a the parish being given six months to provide a school;
  b the introduction of the compulsory education rate, 1870;
  c the passing of the 1902 Education Act.

3.8 STREAMLINING THE ADMINISTRATION OF EDUCATION

By the 1890s it was becoming clear that the administration of education was in a muddle. The leading civil servant of the day, **Robert Morant**, made a powerful attack on the confused and overlapping responsibilities of the central government at Westminster, different government departments and the local School Boards. No fewer than five central authorities were helping to fund education. Besides the Education Department, there was the Charity Commission, and the Admiralty and War Office. In some places, schools were successfully claiming money from the Science and Art Department. Where agriculture was taught, the Board of Agriculture might also give a grant.

Another point of confusion was over the School Boards. In theory, these only had the power under the terms of the 1870 Education Act to raise money for elementary education; but the London School Board was openly going beyond this limitation by sponsoring secondary education. This was confirmed as illegal by the **Cockerton Judgment (1900)**. The whole system was in need of careful reorganization.

The Bryce Commission, 1894–5

The **Bryce Commission** was set up 'to consider what are the best methods of establishing a well-organized system of secondary education in England, taking into account existing deficiencies, and having regard to such local sources of revenue from endowment or otherwise as are available'. The commissioners examined the secondary-school systems of several European countries, the USA, Canada and Australia, and made the recommendations shown in Source A.

SOURCE A

- There should be a **single central authority**, made up of (a) the existing Education Department; (b) the Science and Art Department; and (c) the Charity Commission.

- The central authority should be a **government department** led by a minister. Its aim ought to be 'to bring about among the various agencies which provide that education a harmony and a co-operation which are now wanting'. (In 1899 the **Board of Education** replaced the Education Department. It had authority over primary, secondary and technical education.)

- A **local authority** should be set up in every county and county borough for secondary education of all kinds, and supported by a rate aid.

The recommendations of the Bryce Commission.

The recommendations of the Bryce Commission greatly affected the development of secondary education by defining what aspects should come under central control, and what under local control. As a result of its findings, in 1899 a new **Board of Education** replaced the Education Department. This new body had power over primary, secondary and technical education. Other proposals of the Bryce Commission were acted upon in the **1902 Education Act**, which tried to sort out the chaos by defining exactly what matters were now to come under the control of the new Local Education Authorities.

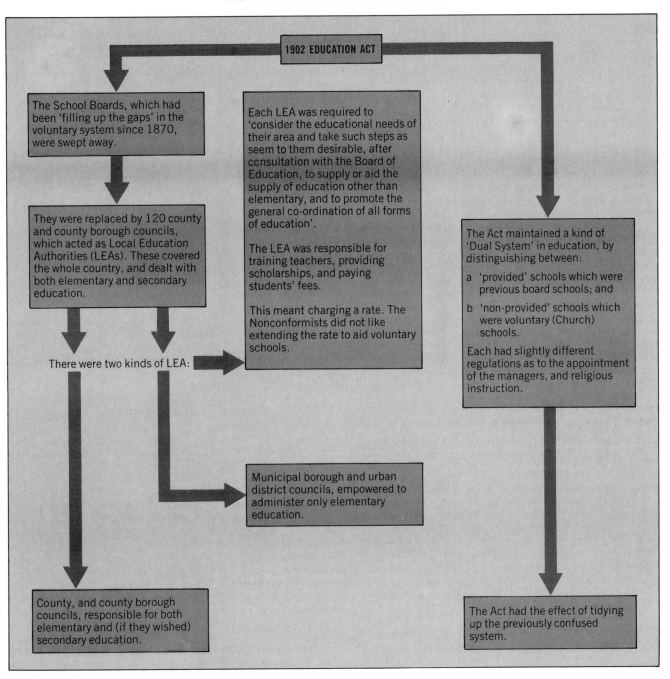

1902 EDUCATION ACT

The School Boards, which had been 'filling up the gaps' in the voluntary system since 1870, were swept away.

They were replaced by 120 county and county borough councils, which acted as Local Education Authorities (LEAs). These covered the whole country, and dealt with both elementary and secondary education.

There were two kinds of LEA:

Each LEA was required to 'consider the educational needs of their area and take such steps as seem to them desirable, after consultation with the Board of Education, to supply or aid the supply of education other than elementary, and to promote the general co-ordination of all forms of education'.

The LEA was responsible for training teachers, providing scholarships, and paying students' fees.

This meant charging a rate. The Nonconformists did not like extending the rate to aid voluntary schools.

The Act maintained a kind of 'Dual System' in education, by distinguishing between:

a 'provided' schools which were previous board schools; and

b 'non-provided' schools which were voluntary (Church) schools.

Each had slightly different regulations as to the appointment of the managers, and religious instruction.

Municipal borough and urban district councils, empowered to administer only elementary education.

County, and county borough councils, responsible for both elementary and (if they wished) secondary education.

The Act had the effect of tidying up the previously confused system.

3.9 FRESH IDEAS AND NEW METHODS

CHANGE

As early as the 1890s the sisters **Margaret and Rachel McMillan** had started campaigning in Bradford on behalf of children's welfare. School medical inspection and the provision of school meals for the undernourished were their top priorities. The McMillan sisters also campaigned for the building of school baths and for camp schools, such as the one they set up at Deptford, London, in 1914.

There was a new awareness of the need to provide a healthy learning environment for the child. This change in approach was due to two main factors: first, the activities and strength of feeling of philanthropists, politicians and educators; and secondly, the force of public opinion, which had been frightened into wanting reform. A large number of young men expecting to be recruited as soldiers in the Boer War had been rejected on the grounds of poor health, and a *Report on Physical Deterioration* (1904) published afterwards highlighted the problem.

The Education (Provision of Meals) Act 1906 permitted LEAs to lay on **free school meals** for children 'unable by reason of lack of food to take full advantage of the education provided for them'. A local rate of up to ½d (1p) in the £ could be charged. The Act did not force LEAs to provide meals, and school catering did not develop fully until 1941. It was war once again that provided the spur to action, when the government was very concerned to keep youngsters fit and healthy.

The **School Medical Service**, at first rejected by the House of Lords largely because of cost, was set up in 1907. LEAs had to give medical inspections to children when they began elementary school, and at times during their stay. In 1918 secondary-school medical inspections were introduced. The LEAs were not called upon to provide medical *treatment* until 1921, when it became a positive duty. At first the government was possibly reluctant to go further because it was afraid of upsetting private doctors. Since then, the system has been expanded to include the provision of school nurses and dentists.

New teaching approaches

The traditional framework within which children were taught was one of learning as a member of a well-organized class with strict rules to obey. In the first quarter of the twentieth century, however, there were experiments in the direction of giving pupils greater freedom. **Maria Montessori**, an Italian doctor of medicine, was a pioneer in this movement. She wanted to provide her pupils with more opportunity to learn through their own experimenting and discovery. So she designed pieces of apparatus which the children could use without any guidance. Montessori was criticised by some as being too 'go as you please', abandoning her proper authority as a teacher and simply letting children teach themselves.

For **A. S. Neill**, on the other hand, Montessori's methods did not go far enough. Neill was against rules of any kind, believing that children were normally good and well-meaning. He was in favour of children being left to their own devices. No attempt

SOURCE **A**

East Peckham pupils, pre-1901.

SOURCE **B**

East Peckham pupils, 1929.

SOURCE **C**

East Peckham pupils, 1985.

would be made to 'mould', and no apparatus would be provided. 'Let children be themselves. Don't force them to do anything', Neill recommended. Lessons were optional at his school, Summerhill, and there was no discipline or authority, which, he believed, only caused fear.

Like Montessori, Neill adopted a 'child-centred' approach. Both first took children's interest and enthusiasm, and then helped them towards self-development through a process of mutual co-operation.

ACTIVITY

Use the three photographs of pupils at East Peckham School, Kent (Sources A, B and C), to complete the table below.

	1929	1985
Class size		
Pupils' clothing		
State of health		
Probable standard of living		

EXERCISE

1 A **change** is a completely new departure from existing practice. A **development** is an extension of an idea or a trend; elements of the old situation can be found in the new. Copy out the partly completed table below. Decide whether each event is a *change*, or a *development* from earlier practice.

Event	Change (C) or development (D)	Reasons
Local Education Authorities were set up (1902)	C	School Boards had administered some schools, and the church the remainder before this date. The LEAs were new in that they administered both.
LEAs *had* to provide free meals for poor children (1941)		
Maria Montessori designed apparatus for free expression		

2 'In history, a few things change, but most things stay the same.' From your study of the photographs of East Peckham children during the last hundred years, say whether you agree or disagree with this conclusion.

3.10 SECONDARY EDUCATION FOR ALL

Most children still went only to an elementary school. At 13, their schooling ended, and they were put out to work. Most parents could not afford – or were unwilling – to pay the fees necessary for a secondary-school place for their child. However, under the new **Free Place System**, introduced in 1907, children could try for a scholarship to a grammar school. There were originally 47,000 of these free places, a number that went up to 60,000 in 1913 and 143,000 in 1927. Children who failed to win a grammar-school scholarship might get a free place in a **central school**. These tended to offer more practical subjects than grammar schools.

The idea was that secondary schools would now be open to children of all social backgrounds. Yet in practice many people were suspicious of allowing working-class children into these schools. Even so, the number of free places increased. In an effort to select children for these places greater use was made of intelligence tests.

The **1918 Education Act** was one of a large group of reforms aimed at helping Britain recover after the First World War. The Bill was introduced to Parliament by **Dr H. A. L. Fisher**, a leading historian, who had left his post at Sheffield University in 1916 to become president of the Board of Education. Fisher had two main criticisms of the education system. First, he felt that too little attention was being paid to bright pupils, who were usually rushed to the top of the school, to spend two or three years in the top class, with nothing further to do. Secondly, he thought that school life was too short; he recommended extra schooling one day a week when youngsters had started work.

Under the Act, education was made compulsory for all up to 14 years old, and LEAs were permitted to raise the leaving age to 15. A new Standard VIII was created for bright pupils.

The out-of-school employment of children up to the age of 14 was restricted. They could not be employed on any school day during school hours, nor before 6 a.m., nor after 8 p.m. Children under 12 were forbidden to work at all. A system of part-time continuation schools, along German lines, was supposed to be set up for children leaving elementary schools. They were to attend these for eight hours per week until they were 18. The curriculum was to have a bias towards local industry. But not all local authorities were able to fund continuation schools in the Depression of the 1920s.

The 1926 Hadow Report and after

The 1918 Act had done nothing to change the way children were transferred from elementary to secondary school at the age of 13. However, Sir W. H. Hadow, Dr R. H. Tawney and Dr Ernest Barker, the main forces behind the **1926 Hadow Report**, believed that the change to secondary school ought to be made at 11. This was to coincide with the 'tide which begins to rise in the veins of youth at the age of 11 or 12, called by the name of adolescence.' Their report was, in fact, given the title *The Education of the Adolescent*.

After the 1918 Education Act

80% go to elementary school only (5–14)

The Hadow Report in theory

All go to primary school (5–11).

The Hadow Report in Practice (1939)

33% of pupils still go only to elementary school.

20% go to elementary school and on to secondary school, some pay, some get free places.

All go on to secondary school (some to grammar schools, some to central schools).

66% of pupils go on to some form of secondary school.

The Hadow Report proposed to call all forms of education up to the age of 11 **primary education**. Education after the age of 11 was to be known by the general name of **secondary education**. Three different kinds of children were identified at secondary level. First, there were those who were academically minded; these were to go to a secondary school at the age of 11+. Secondly, pupils who were of above-average ability were to go to a central school. Thirdly, for the non-academic remainder, there would be a place at a senior school. The report also recommended the raising of the **school-leaving age** to 15 years.

In common with Dr Fisher, the report's authors favoured a system of promotion at school by age rather than by ability. This new system was gradually introduced (Source A).

SOURCE A

Pre 1926	After Hadow	
Standard VII — Very bright of all ages	5th form	Age 15+
Standards V and VI — Bright of all ages	4th form	Age 14+
Standards III and IV — Average of all ages	3rd form	Age 13+
	2nd form	Age 12+
Standards I and II — Dull of all ages	1st form	Age 11+

School classes, before and after the Hadow Report.

In 1938 the **Spens Report** recommended the expansion of free secondary education for all. It proposed a 'tripartite system', consisting of **grammar**, technical and **modern schools**. Children would undergo **intelligence tests** to determine which school they were most suited to. The 1938 report stressed that all schools should be thought of as providing an equally good education, with comparable staff and equipment. They would differ only in being geared towards children with different abilities and needs.

3.11 FURTHER AND ADULT EDUCATION

There was very little adult education, as far as we know, before the nineteenth century. The exception was a few classes of youths and adults, who were taught basic literacy. The Society for Promoting Christian Knowledge backed evening schools for adults in 1711, though only the Welsh circulating schools, under Griffith Jones, approached anything like a system. Evening experiments were also undertaken in Nottingham and Bristol, and by the Birmingham Sunday Society (1789).

With the Industrial Revolution, many adults began to regret that they had not been to school. During the first half of the nineteenth century, to meet this need, adult education became much more common. It also expanded in scope, to offer simple arithmetic as well as reading and writing.

After 1850, the number of these adult schools began to fall. There were several different reasons for this. First, good teachers were not attracted to the work, or the pay offered. Secondly, the upper and middle classes were critical of teaching the poor to read and write. Finally, the need for adult schools was less urgent now that more and more children were receiving an elementary education.

When, in 1800, **Dr George Birkbeck** proposed to lecture on experimental physics to audiences of Scottish mechanics, he was laughed at. 'The mechanics would not come; if they did come they would not listen; and if they listened they would not understand,' went the joke of the time. But Birkbeck's experiment was a great success: 'An audience more orderly, attentive and apparently comprehending I never witnessed.' Birkbeck moved to London and founded the **Mechanics Institute** in 1823, which is now a college of the University of London, for evening and part-time students.

Industrial cities such as Leeds and Liverpool were quick to follow the London example, and by 1850 there were over 600 such institutes in England. With their strong connections with industry, commerce and engineering, mechanics' institutes gave ordinary workers a chance to improve their understanding of the world. By the 1860s the students, who had originally been mechanics, began to come from the middle class, and many of the institutes had their own public libraries.

The modern period in adult education began with the **University Extension Movement**. The idea behind this was simple. If the students could not be brought into the universities, then the universities would bring university teaching to them. Again the initiative came from a Scot, **James Stuart**, who persuaded Cambridge University to organize lecture centres in Derby, Leicester and Nottingham in 1873. The Universities of London and Oxford both created extension societies within five years.

An important consequence of the university extension work was the growth of many of the modern provincial universities, which today still maintain their departments of adult education.

The **Workers' Educational Association** (WEA) was founded in 1905. It has been described as 'the most important agency for

The Leeds Mechanics Institute, 1850.

SOURCE B

A travelling library, belonging to the Warrington Mechanics Institute, 1860.

adult education in the last half-century'. It attracted vast numbers of working men, and later women too, and helped to change ideas about adult education. The WEA's founder was **Albert Mansbridge**, who had wide experience of different kinds of adult education, especially evening classes and university extension. He had also taught typewriting and social history at a London School Board evening school.

R. H. Tawney, who was appointed tutor at Longton, Staffordshire, was one of the WEA movement's leading figures. He introduced a 'discussion hour' into his tutorials.

After the Second World War, there were 900 WEA branches, with over 100,000 men and women coming to classes. Many of the students were manual workers, married women or nurses, all of whom had left school at 15. At first the WEA had been intended to attract only trade union members; but, as subjects such as biology, geology, music, economics, history, literature, philosophy and psychology were introduced, the classes, like the mechanics' institutes before them, began to appeal to a greater cross-section of society. Today, the WEA gets a lot of support from public funds but it is strictly speaking still a voluntary organization.

Further education also came to be organized by post. **Correspondence colleges** were established to satisfy the needs of students who found it impossible to attend classes in person. The first was the University Correspondence College (founded in 1887). Wolsey Hall, Oxford, followed in 1894, and today it prepares students all over the world for degrees, diplomas and certificates, while they work at home at their own pace.

There is no single 'system' in further education today. Rather, it is a network of institutions, courses and qualifications. In the late 1980s the government announced plans to strengthen the **colleges of further education** by making them more independent from the Local Education Authorities and giving them greater financial self-management. In September 1987 the government launched a 'college of the air', the **Open College**, operating through Channel 4 television broadcasts. The idea behind the Open College is to train and upgrade the skills of Britain's workforce to help the country compete against its industrial competitors.

CAUSATION

4.1 THE 1944 EDUCATION ACT

The shape of education in Britain today is in important ways the product of the **1944 Education Act**. There were three main factors, or causes, which produced the 1944 Act.

First, there was a need for a better-trained workforce, so that Britain could compete more effectively with its industrial rivals, especially the USA, Germany and Japan. **Industrial rivalry** with these countries had existed for several generations, and so it should perhaps be considered a *long-term* cause.

Secondly, the government wanted to extend **intelligence testing** to children. It had begun such tests with thousands of army and navy recruits during the Second World War. This was quite a *short-term* cause.

The third factor was the outstanding skill, enthusiasm and determination of one person, the Education Minister **R. A. Butler** who expertly steered the Bill through the House of Commons. This special factor – Butler's presence and abilities – brought the Act into being in 1944, rather than at some other time, and might be described as a *trigger*.

Many of the main features of the 'Butler Act' had been foreshadowed in the 1926 Hadow Report. Under the Act, the education system was reorganized into three stages: **primary education**, **secondary education** and **further education**. The idea of 'elementary education' as an inferior kind of schooling for the poorer classes was swept away.

R.A. Butler, 1902–82, Minister of Education 1941–5

1902	Born in India. Educated at Marlborough School and Pembroke College, Cambridge.
1926	Married Sydney Courtauld (died 1954).
1929	Elected Conservative MP for Saffron Walden, Essex.
1932	Under-Secretary to India Office.
1937	Under-Secretary to Ministry of Labour.
1938	Under-Secretary to Foreign Office.
1941–5	Minister of Education, and architect of 1944 Education Act (the 'Butler Act').
1945–51	In Opposition.
1951–5	Chancellor of Exchequer in Churchill's government.
1955	Lord Privy Seal and Leader of the House.
1957–62	Home Secretary under Harold Macmillan: prison reforms and laws on betting.
1962–3	Deputy Prime Minister, with responsibility for the Common Market and Central Africa.
1963–4	Foreign Secretary under Alec Douglas-Home.
1964	Resigned from active party politics, to become Master of Trinity College, Cambridge.
1965	Created a life peer, 'Lord Butler of Saffron Walden'.
1982	Died.

Secondary education was provided free of charge to all children over 11 years of age. Education would take into account the 'age, aptitude and ability' of the individual child. In this, the recommendations of the recent Norwood Committee (1943) were followed. That committee had concluded that there were three different types of youngster, each of which was suited to a different kind of school. A new examination, the '**11-plus**' would be used to decide which group each child belonged to:

- Those children who were 'interested in learning for its own sake', and who could 'grasp an argument or follow a piece of connected reasoning' would be suited to the more academic work being done in a **grammar** school.
- Those children 'whose interests and abilities lie markedly in the field of applied science or applied art' would be best provided for in a **technical** school.
- And those children who coped 'more easily with concrete things than ideas' were to go to the **modern** school.

The leaving age at each school was to be raised to 15 from 1947.

The 'dual system' of church schools (whether 'aided', 'controlled' or under 'special agreement') and LEA schools would continue. Religious education from now onwards was to consist of a daily assembly and a timetabled lesson.

The Act promised nursery schools but did not make them compulsory. It also introduced grants, helping young people from whatever background to go to college or university.

Many people soon began to argue that the tripartite system of secondary education was too rigid, and that not all children could realistically be placed in one of the three groups. Also, the schools did not seem to have an equally good reputation, after all. The grammar schools were being given more resources, while the secondary moderns were fast becoming the 'poor relation'. And the system did not allow for promotion after a child had been tested at 11.

Experiments with various forms of 'comprehensive education' had proved successful before 1944. The new Labour government of 1945 recommended flexibility and continued experimentation in 'the real interests of the children' (see Unit 4.2).

EXERCISE

1 In your own words, describe the three causes given in the text for the 1944 Education Act.

2 'The most important cause of the Act was Butler's determination that there should be such an Act.' Do you agree with this statement? Give reasons for your answer.

3 The 1902 Education Act followed the end of the Boer War. The 1918 Education Act followed the First World War. The 1944 Education Act became law after the Second World War. Is this just chance, or is war an important cause of change in education? Explain your answer.

4 Do you think that the success of 'scientific intelligence testing' during the Second World War meant it was inevitable that there would be a system of education that divided pupils into different types according to the results of tests? Give reasons for your answer.

4.2 THE COMPREHENSIVE DEBATE

Increasingly in the late 1940s and early 1950s, the 11-plus examination was attacked. The examination was said to be biased in favour of children with middle-class backgrounds. The secondary-modern schools were admitting an overwhelming number of working-class children, while the grammar schools were mainly filled by middle-class children. Also, children stood more chance of passing the 11-plus in some parts of the country than in others. In Wales more than one-third of children were going to grammar schools, but in Surrey only one in seven were selected.

Around this time, a new system began to develop: **comprehensive education**. The idea behind comprehensive schools is that all children, of whatever ability and background, should be educated together in one kind of school. Comprehensive schools were first introduced under the Labour government of the early 1950s. Kidbrooke School, near Lewisham, London, was a famous early example. Similar experiments, avoiding selection at 11, followed in Leicestershire, Croydon and the West Riding of Yorkshire. By the 1960s, most education authorities were abandoning 11-plus selection in favour of comprehensive schooling.

Soon after the Labour victory in the 1964 general election, Antony Crosland, Secretary of State for Education and Science, issued the famous **Circular 10/65: *The Organization of Secondary Education***. The circular asked LEAs to submit plans within a year for changing their secondary schools to comprehensives and abandoning selection at 11. Six main forms of reorganization were recommended (see Source A). By the time the Labour government lost the general election in June 1970, comprehensive schemes had been approved for 129 out of 163 LEAs.

SOURCE B

'22 per cent of army recruits were wrongly placed by the 11-plus.'

Crowther Report, 1959.

SOURCE C

'A far higher proportion of middle-class than of working-class children succeed at the 11-plus.'

Robbins Report, 1963.

SOURCE D

'To achieve genuine equality of educational opportunity, we require to reorganise the state secondary schools on comprehensive lines.'

Signposts for the Sixties, 1961.

SOURCE A

1 The 'orthodox', age 11–18, comprehensive school.
2 A two-tier system for all pupils: age 11–13+ and 13+–18.
3 A two-tier system where all pupils would go to a junior comprehensive school until 13+. Some pupils would then go to a senior school until 18, the rest staying until 15+ at the same school.
4 A two-tier system where all pupils would go to a junior comprehensive until 13+, when all would go to the senior school of their choice.
5 The age 11–16 comprehensive school, followed by a sixth-form college.
6 The 'middle school,' age 8+ until 12+, followed by a comprehensive until age 18.

Types 3 and 4 are not genuine comprehensive arrangements, and were designed only as a temporary measure.

The main forms of comprehensive organization recommended in Circular 10/65.

SOURCE E

Anti-selection message, 1970.

SOURCE

YOUR CHILD'S EDUCATION

UNDER
THE
CONSERVATIVES

UNDER
THE
SOCIALISTS

Political poster, 1971.

Not everyone agreed with comprehensive education, however. There were fears that it would reduce standards. Under the new Conservative government of 1970, Conservative county councils felt safe to ignore introducing comprehensive schools. Voices were raised in favour of the earlier, pre-comprehensive set-up. One of the main criticisms was the damaging psychological effects thought to be produced by large schools of 1,500 to 2,000 pupils. It was feared that bright children would suffer most under the 'all-in' system.

The debate was hotly argued on both sides (see Source B to E and F to H).

SOURCE H

'It would be disastrous if the interests of the most gifted could not be safeguarded. It is perfectly possible to recognise high general intelligence, certainly by the age of 10.'

Eric James, 'Education and Leadership', 1951.

SOURCE I

'Selection has meant that the clever child has been able to work alongside children equally clever, and has therefore gained from pitting his or her mind against a mind of a similar calibre.'

K. Harry Ree, 'The Essential Grammar School', 1956.

SOURCE G

County Hall
March 31, 1971

Dear Parent,

The results of the Secondary Schools Selection Tests for pupils aged eleven plus have now been considered and I am writing to let you know that your son/daughter has not been selected for a grammar school place.

I shall be writing to you shortly to let you know the name of the appropriate secondary modern school which your son/daughter may attend.

Yours faithfully,

Chief Education Officer

QUESTIONS

1 Study Source E. What point is being made?

2 Study Source F. Does this political poster have any connection with the debate over comprehensive and selective schools? Explain your answer.

3 What arguments can be put forward *for* comprehensive education on the basis of the sources here?

4 What arguments can be put forward *against* comprehensive education on the basis of the sources here?

◀ *The kind of letter an education authority would send to inform parents of their child's failure in the 11-plus examination.*

4.3 PUPIL ASSESSMENT

CHANGE

People who run a factory, a business or a shop need to know whether their investment of time and resources has been worthwhile – whether it has produced quality goods or performance. In the same way, when it came to schools, the government was keen that money spent was achieving good results and would justify future spending. The method of checking whether educational aims have been met has traditionally been through **pupil assessment**, or regular testing. Critics of assessment, on the other hand, sometimes argue that testing and examinations make learning a very narrow process (Source B).

One of the earliest forms of pupil assessment also measured the teacher's performance. As we have seen (Unit 3.3), through the system of 'payment by results' (1862), teachers were paid partly according to the attendance level of the children, and partly according to the number of pupils who passed through each 'standard' in the annual examination. The result was that children were drilled into learning very limited information by heart. Inspectors found children holding books upside down, and giving the same answers to questions even when they were asked in a different order.

A standardized **National School Certificate** examination was introduced by the Board of Education into the grammar schools in 1917. It was taken at about 16 years old, and consisted of Latin, English, a modern language, history, geography, mathematics and, for most boys, science. Five credits were taken as a suitable qualification for most jobs. The examination could serve either as a final examination at the end of a pupil's schooling or as a qualification for entering university. In 1922 the **Higher Certificate** examination was introduced for the sixth form. It included advanced science and mathematics, classics or modern studies (business studies), modern languages and geography.

The widespread adoption of intelligence testing during the 1930s and early 1940s resulted in the introduction of the **11-plus** examination in 1944 (see Units 4.1 and 4.2). Opponents of assessment say that it is possible to improve at such tests by having practice at them.

In 1951 the old School Certificate examinations were replaced by Ordinary-level, Advanced-level and, for the best performers, Special-level examinations (O-, A- and S-level). Together these exams formed the **General Certificate of Education** (GCE). Pupils were to be assessed in examinations at the end of their course. The examinations were to be conducted by eight independent examining boards, operated by groups of universities, in the summer and sometimes also during the winter. O-level's were usually taken at the end of a five-year course in a secondary school, and A-level's after a further two years of sixth-form study.

Less academic courses, introducing elements of coursework assessment by the school, were introduced with a new examination, the **Certificate of Secondary Education** (CSE) in 1965. The examination was conducted by fourteen regional boards, schools entering candidates at their nearest board. The

SOURCE **A**

PASS

Hit or miss?

SOURCE **B**

'I'm afraid we don't have much time for teaching here – we're too busy examining.'

The examination obsession?

CSE ability range stretched from pupils who overlapped those taking GCE O-level, down to those of slightly below-average attainment.

Since the early days of the CSE, there was concern about whether it could exist alongside O-level. Some educators thought it was a second-rate examination. Since the early 1970s there have been a number of trial common exams, for the whole ability range. More recently, the Schools' Council has developed a common 16-plus examination in history, and in science, with the examining boards issuing the most able candidates with dual certificates. In 1986–8 the common examination was extended to all subjects in the **General Certificate of Secondary Education** (GCSE), for which children in every secondary school are now entered. At the same time, for each subject a statement of aims, objectives, skills and concepts was drawn up.

SOURCE C

'The Minister of Education, Mr George Tomlinson, announced on April 26 that the present School and Higher School Certificate examinations in Secondary Schools would be discontinued in 1951, when they would be replaced by an examination for a "general certificate of education" open both to boys and girls at school and to candidates not attending school. The main features of the new examination, he said, would be: (1) papers would be set in all suitable subjects at ordinary, advanced, and scholarship levels; (2) all subjects would be optional, no minimum or group requirements being imposed for the certificate; (3) only candidates having a reasonable chance of success should be entered for any part of the examination, and no candidate would be allowed to sit for it who was under 16 on Sept. 1, 1951.'

Extract from 'The Times', May 1948.

SOURCE D

◄ *Three pathways to success and a university place.*

4.4 THE UNIVERSITIES

Up until the beginning of the nineteenth century, the only English universities were **Oxford** and **Cambridge**. Both were in a state of decline, little more than clubs for the idle rich, and were only open to members of the Anglican church. The curriculum was narrow, dominated by the classics.

During the second half of the nineteenth century, the two ancient universities began to respond and adapt to a more industrial society. English, rather than Latin, became the language of discussion; students staying on to do research no longer had to be ordained; and from 1871 Nonconformists were allowed to study for any degree apart from divinity. Most important of all, the curriculum was expanded. New subjects such as natural science, history, law, literature and medieval, modern and oriental languages were introduced, and research was encouraged.

The nineteenth century was also a period of growth. In 1836, the **University of Durham** at last received its **charter** (official recognition), becoming the third English university. Its curriculum resembled that of Oxford and Cambridge, and like them it required students to agree to the Anglican interpretation of Christianity until the repeal of 1871.

Another new development at this time was the building of halls of residence for women students. Yet, despite this, no university was prepared to award degrees to women until the early 1920s.

SOURCE **B**

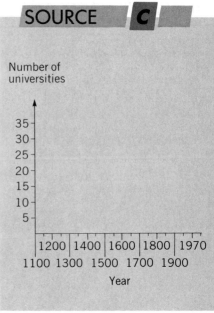

The University of Keele.

SOURCE **A**

Ancient	Nineteenth and early twentieth century	Post-war
Oxford (c. 1185)	Durham (1836)	Nottingham (1948)
Cambridge (c. 1230)	London (1836)	Southampton (1952)
St Andrews (1410)	Wales (1893)	Hull (1954)
Glasgow (1451)	Birmingham (1900)	Exeter (1955)
Aberdeen (1494)	Manchester (1903)	Leicester (1957)
Edinburgh (1583)	Liverpool (1903)	Sussex (1961)
	Leeds (1904)	Keele (1962)
	Sheffield (1905)	Essex (1962)
	Bristol (1909)	Newcastle-upon-Tyne (1963)
	Reading (1926)	York (1963)
		East Anglia (1963)
		Strathclyde (1963)
		Kent (1965)
		Warwick (1965)
		Lancaster (1966)
		Bath (1967)
		Open University (1969)
		Brunel (1968)

Table of universities with their foundation dates.

SOURCE **C**

Number of universities

35
30
25
20
15
10
5

1200 1400 1600 1800 1970
1100 1300 1500 1700 1900
Year

Number of universities in existence in England, Wales and Scotland, 1100–1970.

ACTIVITY

Using the scale shown in Source C, draw a cumulative line graph to show the total number of universities in England, Wales and Scotland at fifty-year intervals from 1100 to 1970. Then identify:

a a period of growth,
b a period of stagnation and
c a period of 'take-off' (rapid development)

in university numbers.

There were calls for a new type of university, without any religious entry requirements, and offering more modern and scientific subjects. The idea was first suggested by a group of educators and writers including Dr Birkbeck, Francis Place and Joseph Hume. Their college, **University College**, opened in 1828 to teach the arts, law and medicine. Oxford and Cambridge were against giving a charter to this new, non-religious 'godless institution' or 'Gower Street blasphemy', as the Anglicans called it. They proposed a rival university, **King's College**, in which religious instruction would be obligatory. By 1836 both colleges were members of the new University of London. The university was given the power to grant **external degrees** to non-resident members; and it had a separate college for women, **Bedford College**, founded in 1849.

During the twentieth century many of the younger colleges have been upgraded to full, independent university status. This has involved a trial period spent as a university college, preparing students externally for London University degrees, followed by the grant of a charter to the college so that it may award its own degrees, and a financial grant from the **University Grants Committee**. These newer institutions are known as the **red brick universities**.

The **Robbins Report (1963)** concluded that there should be more courses which involved the study of more than one subject, especially during the first year. Some modern universities have followed the Keele example, and introduced less-specialized four-year courses.

Ever since the free-place system came into being in the grammar schools in 1907, able pupils, of whatever social background, have had the opportunity of taking up scholarships at secondary school and eventually, through the system of grants, going to university. Nevertheless, recent studies of student admissions show that even today an overwhelming proportion of students are drawn from the middle class, rather than the working class.

The Open University is unique among universities. In 1966 the government proposed a new form of higher education, a 'university of the air', which would extend educational opportunity. Higher education was no longer to be the privilege of a few; it was to be a basic right of all, whatever their personal circumstances. The Open University would 'have an unrivalled opportunity to rectify the long-continuing imbalance' between the sexes when it came to access to higher education – women tied to the home were intended to benefit, and have done so.

The Open University was set up in 1969. It uses a variety of tuition methods, including radio broadcasts, correspondence, group discussion and summer schools. Its greatest impact, however, is through the medium of **television**, and its early morning lectures have proved very successful. It awards both ordinary degrees and honours degrees, obtained by accumulating credits in individual courses following a foundation course.

4.5 EDUCATION IN A MULTICULTURAL SOCIETY

Soon after the Second World War, Commonwealth citizens began to emigrate to Britain. First to arrive during the early 1950s were West Indians. By the end of the decade, immigration had begun to increase from India and Pakistan. The British Nationality Act of 1948 had given Commonwealth citizens the right to free entry and full citizenship in Britain.

By the 1961 Census, over 80 per cent of New Commonwealth immigrants and their descendants were concentrated in urban areas, largely in Greater London, the West Midlands and West Yorkshire.

In 1962 the government passed the Commonwealth Immigration Act to restrict immigrant entry into Britain; but this legislation had only a limited effect as women and children came to join their menfolk who were already in the country. In 1964 the Labour government set up a council to advise the Home Secretary on the housing, education and employment of immigrant school-leavers. Housing and welfare services for immigrants were improved by the Local Government Act 1966.

The **Plowden Report (1967)** drew attention to how some areas of Britain (notably Greater London, the West Midlands and West Yorkshire) were not doing enough to provide suitable schooling for their new citizens. To improve conditions, the report recommended the establishment of **Educational Priority Areas** (EPAs). The idea behind the EPAs was that the government should give extra help to schools in these areas with large minority populations. The report was successful in bringing about four changes: the size of classes was reduced; teachers were given a salary increase in recognition of their extra skills and responsibilities; more cash was available for extra books and equipment; and more nursery education was provided.

In 1967 **Dr A. H. Halsey** was appointed to direct research schemes in Liverpool, the West Riding of Yorkshire, Deptford (London), Birmingham and Dundee – all with large numbers of ethnic-minority pupils (Source A). The research was aimed at identifying skills and approaches that teachers and parents could use to help improve the school performance of under-achievers among ethnic-minority pupils. Particularly successful were summer holiday schools and language programmes.

Many surveys, however, showed that **racial discrimination** still existed in employment, housing and credit facilities. The **Race Relations Act, 1968** tried to put an end to this by prohibiting discrimination on grounds of race. A massive programme for action in housing, education, community and police relations and welfare was proposed in the **Rose Report,** *Colour and Citizenship* **(1969)**. The report included a recommendation that all educational institutions provide courses in the cultures of minorities in Britain.

In 1971 the Conservative government set up playgroup and day-nursery centres, adventure playgrounds and language training centres in ethnic-minority areas. More recently, courses for trainee teachers in **multicultural studies** have been tried out at Sunderland Polytechnic, Bradford and Ilkley College, and

SOURCE **A**

Local Education Authorities in England with over 1,000 ethnic-minority pupils in 1970.

SOURCE **B**

Today's multicultural classroom.

Jordanhill College, Glasgow. The Inner London Education
Authority was one of the first authorities to introduce a
multicultural curriculum and **anti-racist teaching** programmes.

The latest studies indicate that still not enough is being done to
overcome the language barrier, which many people see as the
root of the problem of multicultural education. In 1985, the
Swann Committee reported little enthusiasm for multicultural
teaching among schools in mainly white areas. The evidence,
however, suggests that it is important. For example, the vast
majority of black children aged 13 to 19 in a 1986 study had
difficulty in understanding what their teachers said. More than
half the sample did not place the same meanings on everyday
expressions as a white child would; worse, their teachers were
not aware of this.

Although multicultural education is seen as important by
governments, Local Education Authorities and universities,
there are some people who are against it. Local authorities, while
supporting the principle of educating all children for a
multicultural society, have often been more cautious in putting it
into practice, especially in nearly all-white areas.

4.6 WHO HAS A SAY IN EDUCATION?

Today there are probably three groups which have the right to some influence in the field of education: parents, teachers and the government. This is something relatively new. During the Middle Ages, education came under the responsibility of the church. Then, after the Reformation, governments began to become involved in several countries. In France and Prussia during the Napoleonic period, the state intervened in order to create what it hoped would be strong-willed citizens, who would help bring victory in war. Later, Germany used its education system to become a major industrial power; and more recently Japan has done the same.

In Britain, the idea of government involvement in education, as we have seen, took a long time to be accepted. Most people today, however, take state-directed education for granted as the most efficient way of developing national prosperity and well-being. Since 1944 there has been growing centralization of the education system in England and Wales. The system is directed by a Secretary of State for Education who has almost total power. (See diagram below.)

A say in education: control of the present system.

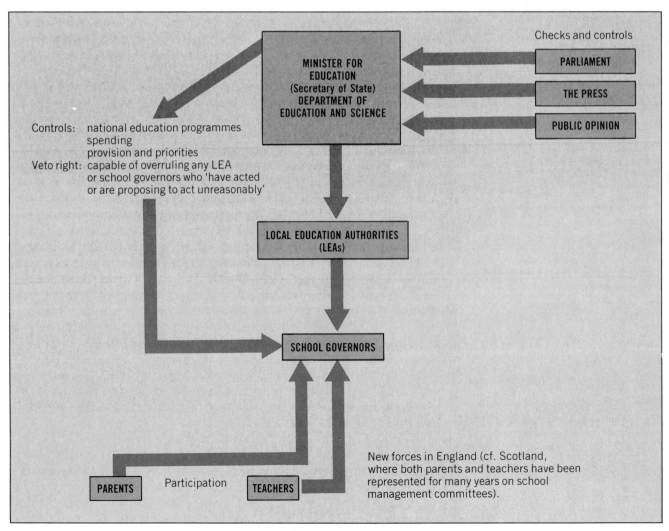

Checks and controls

MINISTER FOR EDUCATION (Secretary of State) DEPARTMENT OF EDUCATION AND SCIENCE

PARLIAMENT

THE PRESS

PUBLIC OPINION

Controls: national education programmes
spending
provision and priorities
Veto right: capable of overruling any LEA
or school governors who 'have acted
or are proposing to act unreasonably'

LOCAL EDUCATION AUTHORITIES (LEAs)

SCHOOL GOVERNORS

New forces in England (cf. Scotland, where both parents and teachers have been represented for many years on school management committees).

PARENTS   Participation   TEACHERS

First rebuffs for advocates of opting out

by Sue Surkes

Two schools in the Conservative-controlled outer London borough of Bromley have guaranteed themselves places in the education history books by failing to secure enough parental support for opting out.

Ravensbourne Girls School became the first to vote against grant-maintained status; the figures 158 for, 432 against, on a 59 per cent turn-out. Ramsden Girls' School in Orpington, Kent, is the first to record a turn-out of less than 50 per cent; only 45 per cent of parents eligible to vote did so. A second postal ballot now has to be held. It will close on January 17.

The idea of a second ballot was introduced by the Government just before the Education Bill became law to calm fears that a well-organized minority of parents might win a vote before anyone else realized what was happening.

As the Act now stands the result of the first ballot is determined by a simple majority of those voting, so long as 50 per cent of the registered parents have taken part. But if less than 50 per cent vote, a second ballot must be held within 14 days of the result of the first ballot. The second ballot is conclusive, irrespective of turn-out.

PARENTS' SAY 'NO' TO CONTINENTAL DAY

Parents have given a hostile reception to the idea of introducing a continental-style day in Kent schools.

Through their governing bodies, they are telling education chiefs that any change to the present system is a non-starter.

An overwhelming majority was totally against it. Several felt the suggestion needed more investigation – but only one delegate was in favour of an 8am start to the school curriculum.

Kent Schools' sub-committee has issued a consultative paper asking for comments on the possible introduciton of a working day whose 8am-2pm timetable is widespread to the continent.

According to the committee, the new structure would incorporate a 20-minute midmorning break and 40 minutes for lunch.

It would embrace eight 35-minute lessons and 30 minutes daily for registration and assembly.

Parent power comes under state control

The Education Act 1944 asserted that the education of each child was to be suited to his age, ability and aptitude. The duty to see that children were so educated was to rest, not on the public authorities, but on their parents. In the 1944 schema, the whole system schools, teachers, governors, local authorities, secretaries of state – was to be seen as a service to children and their parents. The authorities were bound at least to have regard to the (heavily qualified) principle

that children were to be educated in accordance with the parents' wishes, and the courts confirmed that it was the wishes of individual parents, not of some parents' collective, that mattered. In practice, of course, things were not quite so clear (individuality has been trampled down, for example, by public examinations) but at least the law was benign.

Not for long, however. The "consultation document" which the Secretary of State provided for us to

read during August is explicit. It will no longer be enough for the local authorities to see that the opportunities offered to all pupils are "as may be desirable in view of their different ages, abilities and aptitudes" – thus helping individual parents to fulfil their duty. The opportunities, from now on, will have to be "as required by the national curriculum". The responsibility of governors for the curriculum will be abolished.

At all levels of British society today there is a great interest in education. Parents are now much more involved than ever before. They are unlikely to accept without protest conditions in schools that seem to them unsatisfactory, or decisions made by their LEA, child's headteacher or school staff which they feel to be unfair. One strong area of conflict in those parts of the country which still test children at 11 is over the validity of the 11-plus results. The views of many parents have been respected, as with the abolition of all forms of corporal punishment in state schools in 1987.

Parent–Teacher Associations (PTAs) have done much to narrow the gap between school and home. And the **1980 Education Act** has given both parents and teachers greater say in the management of their school's affairs. The Act laid down that all schools with 300 or more pupils had to have at least two elected parent-governors, and at least two elected teacher-governors. Public examination results have to be published in the school's prospectus, and parents are able to take these into consideration when selecting a neighbourhood secondary school.

Parents are likely, under a proposed **Open Enrolment Scheme**, to come into effect in 1989, to have a wider choice still when selecting secondary schools for their children. Under this scheme schools will be able to compete freely against one another, and will be allowed to relax the limit on the number of children they can admit.

At the same time, however, as parents are being given greater influence and more freedom of choice in some areas of education, the Conservative government continues to centralize, and standardize. Two recent proposals are the implementation of a **national core curriculum** for secondary schools, to occupy at least four-fifths of the timetable; and, more controversially, **national testing** at 7, 11 and 14 years old. As part of this centralization policy, the government also intends to encourage selective schools to 'opt out' from comprehensivizing LEA control and to receive funds directly from the Department of Education and Science. In November 1988, Skegness Grammar School became the first school to apply to the Secretary of State for Education to opt out.

QUESTION

Who has the greatest say in education today?

◀ *Some current issues in education.*

INDEX